Fathering
The
Nations

Fatherhood: Raising Generations, Equipping Leaders, and Releasing God's Sons for Effective Works of Service, One Heart at a Time.

Paul L. Graves

PRESS

Dedication

Fathering the Nations is dedicated to Christ Jesus,
the true author and finisher of our faith.

Acknowledgment

I would like to say thank you to my spiritual father, Apostle Dave Viljoen, for training, equipping, raising, and receiving me as his spiritual son. Thank you for all you've done to see that the Christ nature was not only formed but also fashioned in my heart by using yourself as a show and tell model. Apostle Dave, within my heart you are and will forever be seen as my spiritual father.

To Tony Adams, my Covenant Brother in the Lord, thank you for always seeing me for who Christ is, your words of encouragement are forever hidden deep within my heart.

To my mother, Shirley J Graves, I want to say that I love you and that outside of Christ; no one has ever given me more of their time, energy, and love in order to see me succeed in life than you have.

To my loving wife, Tracey, thank you for being so understanding when hours turned into days and days into weeks, as I pushed through in the final stages in order to make sure *Fathering the Nations* was prepared for publication; I love you my Lady!

Table of Contents

Foreword

It has been an honor and my privilege to know Paul Graves as a fellow minister and dear friend for many years. We have co-labored in ministry, traveling to various places in the U.S. as well as in Africa. I have first-hand experience in seeing this son of God grow in times of change as one season of God gave way to another. We have cried and laughed together through the joys and trials of growing up in Christ. We have been the catalysts for one another pertaining to the call of God on our lives. I believe with all of my heart that God the Father has raised up Paul, not only to bring a message of the Fatherhood of God to this generation, but also to be a Father to this generation.

In *Fathering the Nations*, Paul Graves brings forth what the heart of God is saying and doing concerning His plan for His people. Since the beginning of creation, it has always been God's plan to have a family in the earth. *Fathering the Nations* is not about ownership, but about being manifested sons of God. In the pages of this book, you will hear the cry of Hannah's heart for a son. That same cry for the revealing of the manifested sons of God within the earth today needs to be heard throughout the body of Christ. This book communicates God's Passion for His people; it's not about religion, it's about relationship. God is our Father; He's relational, and He communicates with us individually as well as corporately.

May this book, with the empowerment of Holy Spirit, move you with such hunger to know God the Father in a way you have never known Him before? Oh God, give us the cry of Hannah's heart for true sons of God. Let this be a generation that we see the manifested sons of God revealed in your earth. Lord, give us fathers after your own heart, and may we become sons after your own heart.

—Tony E. Adams
Devoted husband and father,
Beloved friend of Paul Graves,
My brother in Christ.

Introduction

Fathering the Nations reveals the character and integrity of Christ that is needed within the heart of God's delegated representatives: apostles, prophets, evangelists, preachers and teachers, in order for the body of Christ to be effectively trained, equipped, and released by God for works of service through Spiritual Fathers "Fatherhood." This book lays a solid foundation of Christ and His Kingdom "living within the hearts of all believers." This book will allow all readers to travel from the known to the unknown, while at the same time never assuming the reader has a full understanding of the material by walking each individual through the book one step at a time.

Fathering the Nations deals directly with the importance of laying a strong biblical foundation to support the overall conclusion for the immediate need throughout all nations to restore the five fold functional offices back to their true mandated commission assigned by Christ Jesus: *Spiritual Fatherhood*. The very definition of Spiritual Fatherhood is the ability to reproduce the nature and character of Christ in the lives of God's sons through raising, equipping, and then releasing God's sons with the ability to operate within their specific function or gifting according to their calling and destiny in Christ Jesus.

For the sake of future generations, church as we know it must also be restored to true Divine Order and Godly Government. *Divine Order*; concerning the biblical patterns and blue prints of our Christian faith, *"Christ-Like"* faith with the practical understanding that as living beings, we are first and foremost sprit; we have a soul, and we live in a body. *Godly Government*; meaning that the government of God is family, family structured, and family based. When we as the Church of Jesus Christ cease being family, we become nothing more than a organization which we simply attend out of a learned behavior full of religious traditions which have been passed down from generation to generation, thus no longer becoming the family of God.

Fathering the Nations deals with the need to establish spiritual father- son relationships throughout the body of Christ through sowing seeds of God's word that will forever establish deep within the heart of both men and women a solid foundation concerning our God-given right to our inheritance in Christ Jesus, through His shed blood at Calvary. *Fathering the Nations* reveals the heart of true fathers and exposes the hearts of false fathers, men and women that have only desired to rule God's people through control and manipulation in the name of religion. This book deals as well with the responsibility of spiritual sons and the ability to make godly decisions concerning their destiny based upon an intimate heart-shared relationship with their creator, Father God.

Fathering the Nations is more then just a book; it is God's literal heart daily beating within mine. I don't believe that this book is a good idea; I believe that it is God's idea. Do I believe that *Fathering the Nations* is a finished or complete work? No, I pray that others will use this book as a catalyst to launch and establish a deeper understanding based upon scriptural revelation revealing godly principles and relationships concerning fatherhood, dealing with fathers, sons and inheritance.

The benefits afforded the readers are the fact that they will not only be challenged but will also gain an understanding of the desperate need for restoring father-son relationships back to the body of Christ. The material in this book teaches one how to clearly distinguish the difference between true and false fatherhood. The readers will gain a clear biblical understanding of those who God has called from birth to fulfill the calling and mandate to be a spiritual father. Within this book, all readers will gain a solid understanding of what it means to walk daily in God's true Divine Order and Godly Government.

Fathering the Nations instills hope in the hearts of all levels of readers through dealing with the frustration and misconceptions concerning leaders within church as we've known it. Those in leadership have never been given authority over the people of God but authority for the people of God. *Fathering the Nations* deals directly with leadership, once again awakening and reestablishing through biblical foundations, God's Divine order for daily living as well as Godly Government for the eternal existence of the true Church of Christ Jesus "*On earth as it is in heaven.*"

Lost within the confines of a historical church lie apostles, prophets, evangelists, teachers, preachers, men and women of God with a pure heart desiring and seeking after truth; though they have been continually denied the knowledge of their true calling in Christ Jesus because of the lack of true spiritual fathers within church as we've known it. So we have apostles recognized and accepted as pastors and appointed by man, and prophets trying to fulfill the functional role of an evangelist because of their boldness and zeal. We've made teachers intercessors and evangelists one man circuses, which must perform every time they are in town. I believe that *Fathering the Nations* is for all levels of readers though it was written as the voice of God to the five-fold ministry gifts throughout the nations. The Church, as we've known it, must change though the only way church as we've known it will change is when leadership as we've known it changes.

—Paul Graves
Founder of Bible to Life Ministries,
Atlanta, Georgia

CHAPTER ONE

Kingdom Principles

It's not hard to see the decline in moral values in the world today. We live in a day and age where the lines between right and wrong seem to be growing harder to distinguish. Monogamous marriage relationships are rapidly becoming the pattern of yesterday, while same sex marriages are more frequently becoming the new pattern for the future. It would be safe to say that according to the moral breakdown in society, in the eyes of most people, they would agree that uncertainty waits around every corner. Remember in times past when moral values and a handshake were all that was required in order to seal a deal? Can you remember when a man would receive employment that would require an honest day's work, for an honest day's pay? Look how quickly our world is declining from these precious values. These are the events that Paul the Apostle spoke of to Timothy, concerning the last days.

> But mark this: there will be terrible times in the last days. People will be lovers of them-selves, lovers of money, boastful, abusive,

disobedient to their parents, ungrateful, unholy, without love, unforgiving, slanderous, without self-control, brutal, not lovers of the good, treacherous, rash, conceited, lovers of pleasure rather than lovers of God—having a form of Godliness but denying it's power. Have nothing to do with them. (2 Timothy 3: 1-4 *NIV*)

Apostle Paul is not saying that what was previously taking place in his generation and that which would continue to progress into future generations, was unchangeable. He understood the godly principal concerning sowing and reaping. He knew that as long as sin was predominantly sowed into the lives of all those upon the earth, the only outcome would be to reap a harvest, based upon what was sown. As God's people choose to sow His seed in the earth *"Righteousness, Peace, Joy,"* the earth will then reap the God harvest, bearing the fruit of the sown seed.

Paul the Apostle also writes to the Church of Romans concerning their wicked deeds. These were people who had been exposed to God's divine nature and power, though still chose to walk in ways that did not lead to life and Godliness. They claimed to be wise, though their hearts were foolish. We learn in *Romans 1:18-28* that the Lord finally gave those who were operating under the spirit of anti-Christ, over to a depraved mind. To be given over to a **depraved mind**, means they were given over to their own natural desires. Anything that is not for Christ is against Christ. Those who refused to conform to the Christ nature were considered to be operating under the control of the "anti-Christ spirit" or "anti-the Christ nature", not pro-Christ.[1]

Mankind Willfully Relinquishes Garden Authority
God fashioned out of the dust of the ground a man,

called Adam.[2] Adam was created in the image of God, *which is spirit.*[3] God's word in the book of Thessalonians refers to His creation as a spirit, having a soul, living in a body.[4] Though sad, within the structure of church as we've known it, we've been taught the exact opposite concerning our priorities for living *"body, soul, and spirit."* The truth is that mankind was created as a spirit being in God, before the foundations of the earth. Even though we now walk in the natural clothed with flesh, we'll forever live throughout eternity created in God's image *"Spirit."* You see, whether we accept or reject Christ, nothing can alter the truth, that either "with God's presence" or "without God's presence", we as spirit beings, will always continue to exist.

> *"Adam was created in God's image along with Eve, who was taken out of the side of Adam."*

> And God said let us make man in our image, and in our likeness, and let them rule over the fish of the sea and the birds of the air, over the livestock, over all the earth, and over all the creatures that move along the ground. (Genesis 1:26 *NIV*)

Notice from this scripture that God not only created mankind in His image, though in His likeness as well, making a clear distinction between the two. *"Church as we've known it,"* has communicated that God's image and likeness are one in the same.

Before their disqualification in the Garden of Eden, Adam and Eve were not only created to walk in the image of God, but with His likeness as well. *Genesis 1:28* says God blessed them and said to them, *"Be fruitful and multiply, increase in number; fill the earth and subdue it, rule over the fish of the sea and the birds of the air and over every living creature that moves on the earth.*" Prior to their disqualification, Adam and Eve walked as God walked which means they walked in full dominion, authority and rulership over everything on the earth.

Adam and Eve were created as eternal beings with the God purpose of procreating and filling the earth with godly offspring, created in God's image and likeness. Although, once both Adam and Eve partook from the tree of the knowledge of good and evil, they had willfully plunged headfirst into disobedience. As a result, both were placed outside the Garden, which was created by God for mankind to live. Through Adam and Eve's lack of trust, they willfully relinquished their God-given rights to live with "**Garden Authority**", leaving it behind in order to be redeemed at a later date. "*Garden authority*", was the ability for both Adam and Eve to trust God completely, based upon their individual intimate relationship with God. The ability to shut the mouth of the serpent was birthed out of their intimate relationship with God. Though yielding to the temptations of the natural man caused both Adam and Eve to lose trust and turn their back on their relationship "covenant" with their creator. The greatest loss to all mankind as a result of the disobedience of Adam and Eve was the separation of natural man from an intimate heart-shared relationship with God, "Garden Authority or God's Likeness"

satan Has Never Had Authority Over Those Who Feared God

One day the angels came to present themselves before the Lord and satan also came with them. The Lord said to satan, where have you come from? satan answered the Lord, from roaming through the earth and

going back and forth in it. Then the Lord said
have you considered my servant Job? (Job
1:6-8 *NIV*)

Although Job believed in God, his authority to render
satan powerless; was diminished. Job was a product of the
fall of mankind, living in a sin-consumed environment. We
need to understand that Job did not have the same authority
over the enemy as Adam and Eve had in the garden, prior to
their disobedience. As we see in this Job passage of scripture, satan was roaming the earth looking for those whom he
could torment with his corrupt spirit and anointing.[5] The
very fact that satan was roaming the earth, proves that he is
not omnipresent or all powerful or all knowing. As well, we
will see in this next segment, that satan had no power over
those that feared God. We've all either read books or heard
teachings concerning the fact that Adam and Eve gave all
authority over to the enemy. The truth is that through their
lack of relationship with God, they simply relinquished or
laid down their God-given authority.

One way to look at this in a practical sense is to say, "I
lost my suntan" you see, the truth is that an individual can
not "lose" a suntan. We all know that it's hard work to maintain a tan; the truth is that it's much harder for some than
others. In order to maintain a suntan, an individual must
continue to expose his or herself to the sun. It's only the lack
of exposure, which allows a suntan to slowly diminish or
fade away. This is the same principal relating to how Adam
and Eve's authority began to fade in the garden. God did not
take away their ability to walk in an intimate heart-shared
relationship with Him. Through their unbelief and lack of
trust they began to gradually move away from an intimate,
heart-shared relationship with God, while still living in the
garden. Once placed outside the garden by God, both Adam
and Eve learned to live all over again, though not only how

to live but how to die. Thus a wall of divide slowly grew between God and mankind called sin.

Though mankind had now lost the likeness of God *"**Garden Authority**, an* intimate, heart-shared relationship", their acts of obedience through faith allowed God the ability to work on their behalf. In the later part of *Job 1:8* after the Lord asked satan if he had considered Job, the reply of satan was "There is no one on earth like him, he is blameless and righteous."

> Does Job fear God for nothing? satan replied "have you not put a hedge around him and his household and everything he has? You have blessed the work of his hands. (Job 1:9-10 *NIV*)

God has always taken care of those who feared Him and patterned their lives after righteousness and holiness. It's important for us to understand that Job lacked the ability to operate in full garden authority *"likeness of God"* over the enemy in his life. His lifestyle toward God, on the other hand, allowed him the ability to rest under the protection of the one he outwardly professed and lived for.[6] Even though mankind slowly relinquished God's likeness through disobedience, it did not mean the enemy now had authority to destroy the lives of those that believed. The fall of man eventually brought with it the removal of God's character and nature in the hearts of mankind. Though the word of God says, *"The righteous have never been forsaken nor their descendants left begging for bread,"*[7] God has always protected those who loved Him and patterned their lives after Him. The earth has always belonged to the Lord. The earth is the Lord's and the fullness thereof. [8]

God has always had a voice throughout the Old Testament and His power has forever been present since the beginning of time.

God was not tempting Job unto sin or even testing Job through sin. God permitted Job's life to be touched by the enemy to bring Job into a deeper, heart-shared relationship with the Lord. This test would bring forth the righteousness and holiness of God within the life of Job greater then he had ever imagined. [9] So you see; satan was used only as a pawn or a puppet in the hands of God, in order to bring forth a greater level of relationship between God and Job. We are still tested today much in the same way. As we hear the word of God and allow the word to become alive within our hearts, this is when God's test is given.

Many things that happen within the lives of the believers today we attribute to the enemy; in actuality it's the Lord touching us in areas that we don't like to be touched. We, as the body of Christ, need to stop giving the enemy more credit then he deserves. The truth is that he deserves no credit, and Christ deserves all the credit, whether good or bad, *"All things work together for good to those that love the Lord and are called according to His purpose."*

Imputed Sin

Since the disobedience of Adam and Eve, a sinful nature **"Imputed Sin"** was born, now flowing through the blood-line of all mankind from birth. We must understand that all mankind is born with imputed sin. This is the sinful nature inherited from disobedient man through an unrepentive heart, which drives man to perform the vile acts that Apostle Paul spoke about in *2 Timothy 3:1-5*. Imputed sin causes mankind's nature to war daily, in direct opposition to the character and nature of Christ Jesus.

Because mankind willfully laid down the likeness of

God, the only way for God to restore His likeness back to mankind was through man "earthen Vessel." The womb of woman is the door, which births mankind into the natural. Jesus Christ is the door through which all must enter, in order for mankind to live in the spirit. The enemy was never birthed through the womb of woman, nor has he ever entered through the door of Jesus Christ in order to walk in the spirit. Thus the enemy is illegally dwelling in the earth; satan has no legal right to live in the earth therefore he has no power and authority over the earth. We must still keep in mind that he is powerful only through deception. Through our lack of relationship with God, we give the enemy the power to operate illegally on the earth. We as men and women born through the door of flesh (Womb of woman) have the legal right to live and have our being in the earth; satan having never legally entered through the womb of flesh is the "Thief and a Robber."

> Verily, verily, I say unto you He that entereth not by the door into the sheepfold, but climbeth up some other way the same is a thief and a robber. (John 10:1-2 *KJV*)

> Then said Jesus unto them again, verily, verily, I say unto you I am the door of the sheep. All that ever came before me are thieves and robbers: but the sheep did not hear them. (John 10:7-9 *KJV*)

Just as we were first born in the natural through the "door" womb of a woman, we are also born spiritually by faith in Jesus Christ. The opportunity for mankind to once again walk in the God nature rested on the man Jesus Christ, *"The doorway to spirit and life."* Once born through the womb of woman, legal entrance into the earth would now allow Jesus Christ the ability to function in full authority and dominion. Thus God sent His only begotten Son wrapped in flesh, born of a woman, in order to legally gain entrance into the earth. Only those born naturally can also be born spiritually, which is the second birth, and carry the power and authority of God.

Regaining Legal Entrance in the Earth

> So the Lord God said to the serpent because you have done this, cursed are you above all the livestock and all the wild animals! You will crawl on your belly and you will eat dust all the days of your life. And I will put enmity between you and the woman, and between your offspring and hers; He will crush your head and you will strike His heel. (Genesis 3:14-15 *NIV*)

Through the womb of woman, God has chosen by His seed to regain legal entrance back into the earth. Scripture teaches us that God established a covenant with a man Abram *"The Abrahamic Covenant."*[10] This covenant, which required Abram's obedience, as well as, sacrificing the shed blood of innocent animals, would give God functional/operational powers in the earth. Just like the marriage covenant empowers a woman to carry her husband's name, giving her power of attorney; the Abrahamic covenant allowed both Abram and Sari to receive natural name change, authorized by God. The changing of both Abram and Sari's name would allow them power of attorney, which was the ability to operate on behalf of God in the earth. The Abrahamic Covenant, like the marriage covenant, gave them power in God, and God legal power in the earth. God joined His name with Abram and Sari in order to set in motion a never-ending promise. God promised to be their father and the father to their children. He chose to establish His covenant with man, knowing that eventually it would bring about the change of heart through salvation, that one day would carry the power to deliver the whole human race out of their sin consumed nature "Imputed Sin"

So God established the Abrahamic Covenant, which consisted of Abram's descendants growing to be as numerous as the stars within the sky and from his seed would come forth deliverance to all nations. God promised Abram that he would be the father of nations and out of his loins Isaac "the son of promise" would arise, in which God's covenant would continue. One of the most significant things that the Abrahamic Covenant entailed was the fact that Abram and his wife Sari both received name change. God showed His desire to be joined with mankind, by joining Himself with both Abram and Sari by placing part of His name into both of theirs *Genesis 17:5. * And God created man in His own image, in the image of God He created him; male and female He created them. *

Abram + **Jehovah** = Abraham   Sari + **Jehovah** = Sarah

Man + **God** = Man of God   Women + **God** = Women of God

No longer was Abram called Abram, but now his new God-given name was Abraham. As well, no longer was Sari called Sari, but her new God-given name was now Sarah. We can see clearly concerning the name change that God was initiating a joining of Himself with mankind. This joining in the natural was only a picture of what was to come in the spirit. Mankind laid down the ability to trust God through an intimate, heart-shared relationship, but God however has forever purposed within His heart to walk as one with mankind.

The seed Jesus Christ that would crush the head of the enemy would come from Abraham's descendants. It was not by chance that Mary the mother of Jesus, was a descendant of Abraham. Thus through the womb of woman legal entrance into the earth would now be regained by God. Through the death and resurrection of His son Jesus Christ, God's nature; that is His likeness, *"heart-shared relationship,"* could now once again be entrusted to His creation, you and I. [11]

Restoring the Likeness of God

Why was the likeness of God restored and to who was the likeness of God restored? These are logical questions that we know many of us have asked at one point or another in our Christian walk. The likeness of God was restored back to His Church so that we as believers could now operate and function as the first Adam prior to his disobedience. [12]

Mankind +God's Likeness = Godliness = God Likeness = Holiness, Righteousness

> So it is written, the first man Adam became a living being, the last Adam a life giving Spirit. The Spiritual did not come first, but the natural and after the natural the spiritual. The first man was of the dust of the earth, the second man from heaven, so also are those who are of heaven. And just as we have born the likeness of the earthly man, so shall we bear the likeness of the man from heaven.
> (1 Corinthians 15:45-49 *NIV*)

Upon the death and resurrection of Jesus Christ, all believers now walk with the likeness of Christ, or the Christ Nature. The godly principle to remember is first the natural and then the spiritual. We must first be conceived and then birthed out of the womb of flesh, which is known as the first birthing, before we can become spiritually born again which is the second birthing. Natural birthing, just as with the first Adam, possesses no power to bring spiritual life. Adam and Eve were commissioned by God to be fruitful and multiply; their multiplication consisted of natural offspring. God's plan in the beginning is still the same concerning today. God still desires natural offspring, though God now also requires spiritual multiplication as well.[13]

Mankind must be restored to God's original plan in the garden, so that we can fulfill God's plan and purposes in the earth. There are several reasons for the creation of mankind. It's vital to understand what our purpose and function as believers in today's world is. The God purposes that we must fulfill are not only natural multiplication, but also multiplying the Christ nature throughout the nations. Apart from the first birthing, which was according to the natural, the second birthing is according to the spirit. To be fruitful and multiply now suddenly seems to take on a whole new meaning.

The last Adam is a life giving spirit. Christ now lives within the hearts of all those who believe. He has freely given every man, woman, and child the ability to enter into His life. Mankind has already been forgiven of all sins; Jesus died once and for all. [14] His death on the cross—followed by His resurrection—was the completion of His ministry. Though all sins are forgiven, not all mankind ask for forgiveness. It's our responsibility to accept Jesus Christ as our redemptive sacrifice. Without accepting the sacrifice of the shed blood of the Lamb, there is no remission for sin. And only through accepting the Blood of Jesus Christ, confessing with our mouth and believing within our heart that Jesus Christ is the son of God "Last Adam", can we be conceived and birthed in spirit through the last Adam.[15] We once bore the likeness of the first Adam, which is the nature of man, or the sinful nature. Now through Christ, the last Adam, we bare the likeness of God, the God nature.

1 Corinthians 15:46 states first the natural then the spiritual, as with relating the old man and the new man. The old man living with imputed sin was continually governed by the natural desires of the flesh: emotions, feelings, and selfish pleasures. The new man lives by the Spirit, obeying the word of God as his or her first and final authority.

> You however are not controlled by the sinful nature but by the Spirit, if the Spirit of God lives in you and if any one does not have the Spirit of Christ, he does not belong to Christ. But if Christ is in you, your body is dead because of sin, yet your spirit is alive because of righteousness. And if the Spirit of Him who raised Jesus from the dead is living in you, He who raised Christ from the dead will always give life to your mortal body through His Spirit that lives in you.(Romans 8:9-11 *NIV*)

"Now through Christ we as believers have the ability to pick up what was once left in the garden thousands of years ago, Garden Authority." It's this authority that will join the heart of God with man, in order for His glory to cover the earth, just as the waters cover the sea "completely."

> Since then you have been raised with Christ, set your hearts on things above, where Christ is seated at the right hand of God. Set your minds on things above not earthly things. For you died and your life is now hidden with Christ in God. When Christ who is your life appears, then you also will appear with Him

in glory. (Colossians 3:1-4 *NIV*)

As born again believers, our focus is now redirected towards a life led by the spirit of God, reflecting the likeness of Christ. Christ's ultimate plan is to appear in His body the living Church, which isn't built by the hands of man, but by Christ himself. His purpose is to manifest His likeness through His Church, you and I. In this book we will learn that redemption is only the beginning of God's plan. It is the birthing of mankind into God's plan.

> For we know that our old self was crucified with Him, so that the body of sin might be done away with, that we should no longer be slaves to sin—because anyone who has died has been freed from sin. (Romans 6:6 *NIV*)

> In the same way count yourself dead to sin but alive to God in Christ.
> (Romans 6:11 *NIV*)

> Do not offer the parts of your body to sin as instruments of wickedness, but rather offer yourself unto God, as though who have been brought from death to life; and offer the parts of your body to Him as instruments of righteousness. For sin shall not be your master for you are not under law but grace. (Romans 6:13-14 *NIV*)

As the sons of God we are no longer indebted to sin; we no longer walk with imputed sin flowing through our veins. No longer do we walk with the old sinful nature, for we have been bought with a price, and therefore been made a new creature in Christ, now carrying the ability to walk in His likeness.

Blood Covenant

As believers, our lives are no longer our own, we now belong to and have a covenant relationship with God our Father through Jesus Christ *Jeremiah 31:31-34.* Father God through the death of His Son has now established a Blood Covenant with man.[16] This is a vital area that's necessary for gaining an understanding of who we are in Christ and the promises that have now been given to all that believe in Jesus Christ, the Son of God. There is no way that we'll be able to scratch the surface concerning the Blood Covenant, though we'll lay a quick and brief foundation so that all the elements will be in place for the rest of this book to be properly built.

What is a **covenant**? *A covenant is a binding agreement between two or more parties.* When different parties enter into a covenant they are saying to one another *"I shall abide by the terms and conditions of this binding agreement, whatever the cost."*

Marriage is an example of a sacred covenant between two parties consisting of a male and female. Both parties in the presence of others vow to one another that they'll stay together for better or worse, through sickness and health, till death do them part. The covenant of marriage must always be presented and conducted as a 100% partnership. The marriage covenant was never designed to function under the terms or conditions of a 50/50 partnership. Both parties involved must give all of themselves for the other. Neither a husband nor wife can afford to withhold any part of themselves, if both desire the success and fulfillment of their marriage vows.

Another example of a covenant of love would be the covenant that was established between David and Jonathan. Both portrayed a love that all believers should show towards one another. David's love for Jonathan was outwardly shown in the presence of all Israel, with every tear that rolled down his cheek and fell to the ground, once the death of both Jonathan and Saul was reported to David. How great was the love and strength of their covenant? David said, *"His love for Jonathan surpassed the love of any woman."*

Many times while during war, different nations or countries depending on the situation will join forces together, although these joining of forces or covenants would only last as long as the conflict. Keep in mind, that there are many types and duration of covenants. Some like the marriage covenant are binding agreements, unto death. Others, such as times of war, are temporal agreements, established only for a time and season.

There are many different reasons that people enter into covenants with one another. Some of the reasons that covenants are established are for protection *"security,"* as the example we had previously discussed concerning times of war. We see in *Genesis 21:22* that Laban's motives for establishing covenant with Jacob was only for security. Another reason for establishing a covenant could be related to business, two or more parties joined together to increase their financial status. Also many covenants have been made out of love for one another, just as we have also previously given an illustration concerning the institution of marriage and the covenant bond between David and Jonathan.

Now that we have a very simple understanding of what a covenant is and some different types of covenants and why we would consider entering them, let's talk about the most sacred covenant of all, the ***Blood Covenant**, the everlasting covenant.*

God has chosen to establish His Blood Covenant within the hearts of mankind. God's Blood Covenant is an eternal binding agreement between two parties, God and mankind. The terms of this eternal binding agreement is the fact that everything God has He freely gives to man, and all that man has we freely give to God. Each joining party must contribute 100% in order to ensure the success of the Blood Covenant. How many of you know that God has everything to offer mankind, and we on the other hand have nothing to offer God? Also according to the terms of the Blood Covenant, all that God owes, man owes, as well as all that man owes God owes. The truth is that God owes nothing, and man owes everything. Jesus Christ who knew no sin became sin so that mankind could be redeemed from their sinful nature. God's covenant was established through the actual shedding of the blood of Jesus Christ, God the Son.

God paid the full price, though mankind must still receive Jesus Christ as Lord and Savior in order to activate this eternal covenant established through the shedding of royal blood. God's Blood Covenant is the only way for mankind to ever walk in the life changing power of Christ, and to function in true God-given authority to heal the sick, mend the broken hearted, and set the oppressed free from the chains of the enemy. No longer would the blood of animals be required for the temporal covering of sins. Jesus has now become our sacrificial lamb. He willfully chose to lay down His life as our eternal sacrifice, openly destroying the power of sin and death once and for all.

Anointed One

> The spirit of the Lord is upon me because He has anointed me to preach good news to the poor. He has sent me to proclaim freedom for the prisoners and recovery of sight for the blind, to release the oppressed, to proclaim the year of the Lord's favor. (Luke 4:18-19 *NIV*)

This New Testament scripture was the fulfillment of the prophetic word spoken in the book of *Isaiah 61:1-2*. Jesus Christ is the anointed one, the fulfillment and completion of Old Testament prophecy. The Old Testament was a type and shadow of Jesus Christ, continually paving the way and pointing the direction toward the Messiah.

In reading scripture, we find that the Son of God was always referred to as Jesus Christ, prior to the death, burial and resurrection. The name Jesus Christ describes His functional role as God the man, representing humanity while upon the earth. Jesus was natural man walking with the eternal Christ alive and dwelling on the inside. Jesus represented humanity, the human race. Christ represents the nature of the deity – all-powerful, all knowing, omnipresent God. Jesus, the man, alone was powerless to bring about the salvation of the world without the Christ nature dwelling on the inside. Therefore a joining of both humanity and deity was required, and His name was Jesus Christ or Jesus the Christ.

After the resurrection of Jesus Christ, we find that scripture refers to the Son of God as Christ Jesus. God's Son has now taken His rightful and functional role as "Christ", seated at the right hand of His Father.

> Believe me when I say that I am in the Father and the Father is within me: or at least believe on the evidence of the miracles themselves, I tell you the truth, anyone who has faith in me will do what I have been doing. He will do even greater things then these because I am going to the Father. And I will do whatever you *ask in my name*, so that the Son may bring glory to the Father. You may ask of me anything *in my name* and I will do it. (John 14:11-14 *NIV*)

While Jesus was functioning as natural man on the earth, those who believed could not experience the full power and authority of the spirit of Christ, *"living within their hearts"*, until the resurrection. The key in this scripture is the fact that Jesus said that we would do greater works than He had done. Why? He was going to His Father. The likeness of Christ or the Christ nature was dispersed upon and within all believers as a direct result of His death and resurrection.[17] This releasing of God's spirit into the hearts of all who believe, was the beginning of the ministry of Christ Jesus. To this ministry there is no end; for even today Christ is at work within the lives of those who believe. Now we, as believers, have the ability through the Anointed One-the Christ *"living within our hearts"*, to perform greater works than Jesus. We are not greater than Jesus, nor are we Jesus, though just as Jesus represented humanity through His natural birth, we also represent humanity. Just as Christ represented deity within the physical body of Jesus, so is the Christ, represented by the Holy Spirit, in the physical body of all believers today.

*"I will do whatever you ask **in my name**, so that the Son may bring glory to the father. You may ask of me anything **in my name** and I will do it. John 14:14."*

There is no power within the utterance alone, of the name of Jesus; not once in scripture did Jesus ever speak forth His natural name to manifest the power of God. It was the understanding of the character and authority within Jesus that openly display God's love and power towards those He came in contact with. This character and authority is Christ, the eternal God living within the heart of natural man. Jesus said, *"I only do what my Father tells me."* As man, Jesus had the ability to hear the voice of father God, with the understanding that God's spirit was dwelling within His heart, and yielding Himself to God's spirit *"Christ."*

The definition of **name** speaks of an *understood character and authority*. Let's use an individual's last name as an example. It's not the letters or pronunciation of a last name that gives one power over people or nations, but the understanding of both the character and authority of that last name, which is acknowledged by others. Only when we as individuals understand who we are and the rightful benefits of carrying a particular last name, can we begin to walk in the authority of that name. This is the same concerning the name of Jesus. It's not the letters or pronunciation alone of the name Jesus, which enables believers to walk with God-given authority and perform greater, works then Jesus. The power that we as believers carry is manifested when we gain an understanding of the character and authority of Christ, living within our hearts.

"There is power in the name of Jesus, though the power comes from a people who know who they are in Christ, and who Christ is in them."

Many people have placed their focus on the man or name Jesus without an understanding of the Christ, *God's character and authority*. If we focus on the representation of humanity based upon the physical name of Jesus and fail to gain an understanding of the anointed one "Christ," we are no better than the Scribes and Pharisees. Both recognized Jesus the man by name, though denied the character and authority of God "**the Christ**," "*Having a form of Godliness though denying the power of God.*" As Christians we must not deny the truth concerning Christ "the King of glory," who now dwells within the hearts of all those who believe.

Generation of Christ
God has called each one of His sons to walk according to His spirit, which will empower us to begin operating and

functioning in true God-given power and authority. In this next segment we'll be branching out into some deeper waters concerning who we are in Christ. I'd ask that you put on your spiritual eyes and ears so that we'll come into this section willing to receive and become challenged by the Holy Spirit.

Matthew 1:1-17 speaks of the genealogy of Jesus the man; in this portion of scripture we see the generations listed starting with Abraham and ending with Jesus. If you count the descendants from verses 1-16 in Matthew, it appears that there are forty-one generations including Jesus. Let's take a close look at verse 17.

> Thus there were fourteen generations in all from Abraham to David, to the exile of Babylon, and fourteen from the exile to the Christ. (Matthew 1-17 *NIV*)

Upon adding up all the generations from verse 1 through verse 16 we seem to come up with forty-one generations. Now if we take a look at verse 17 in Matthew and add up the three sets of fourteen generations, we come up with forty-two generations. Could it be possible that the scriptures had contradicted themselves, which would make the word of God fallible? Not likely, because the word of God is the Logos, which is the infallible, never changing word of God. So where did the forty-second generation come from, and who are they?

We as believers "the bride of Christ"; are the forty-second generation "sons of God." Jesus "son of man," representing humanity was the forty first generation. I'd also like to challenge you with the truth that God's Church was birthed in Christ, out of the side of Jesus Christ while upon Calvary.

> Praise be to the God and Father of our Lord Jesus Christ! In His great mercy He has given us new birth into a living hope through the resurrection of Jesus Christ from the dead. (1Peter 1:3 *NIV*)

Where the first Eve was birthed in the natural from the first Adam, the last Eve, the bride of Christ, God's Church, was birthed in the spirit out of the womb or wound in the side of Jesus Christ "last Adam."

New Jerusalem, God's Corporate Body Made Up Of Many Members

> I saw the Holy City the New Jerusalem coming down out of heaven from God prepared as a bride beautifully dressed for her husband. And I heard a loud voice from heaven saying now the dwelling of God is with men. And He will live with them, they will be His people and God Himself will be with them and be their God. (Revelations 21:2-3 *NIV*)

As believers we are the bride beautifully dressed for our husband, Christ Jesus. We must ask ourselves the question: Did Jesus Christ die on the cross of shame and arise on the third day for a Holy City that will perish, or for a City whose maker is God? A City built with living stones, with eternal hands, the hands of God.

> For he was looking forward to a city with foundations, whose architect and builder was God. (Hebrews 11:10 *NIV*)

According to *Hebrews 11:10*, God allowed Abraham a glimpse into the future, and he saw the Holy City, the New Jerusalem, the last Eve and the Bride of Christ, *"God's Church, You and I."*

> Awake, Awake O Zion clothe yourself with strength. Put on your garment of splendor, O Jerusalem, the Holy City the uncircumcised and defiled, will not enter you again.(Isaiah 52:1 *NIV*)

As Zion we need to clothe ourselves with strength and put on the garment of splendor, which speaks of God's glory, for no more can imputed sin *"sinful nature"* defile us, for we are now the bride of Christ.[18] As the bride we are to be led and ruled by the spirit of the living God " the Holy Spirit." We have heard it for years in songs and sermons that we are marching to Zion; the truth is that were not marching to Zion; Zion, the dwelling place of God, is marching.

Zion represents the dwelling place of God in the spirit, and we as blood bought saints of God have now become His ***"Holy Habitation."***

CHAPTER TWO

Why Fatherhood

In today's society, as technology around the world continues to advance forward, it would seem to appear as though godly principles and honest moral values are sadly decreasing within the hearts of mankind.[19] Just as I've stated in the first chapter, there's a strong breakdown of moral and ethical structure throughout the world. We live in times where it's considered an inconvenience for families to stay together and persevere through life's unexpected ups and downs. The heart of family structure has been violently infiltrated by the lying, seducing spirit of the enemy, which as we've seen or experienced, only leads to destruction and devastation. There is hope for this generation, and many generations to come, though our hope is solely found in Christ Jesus, our risen Savior. Now by His spirit, Christ lives within the hearts of all who believe upon His name. I could sit and write all day concerning the problems of the world, although I'd rather write concerning the solutions. We need to gain solid understand right here in the beginning of this next chapter. God's purpose through creation was to establish for Himself a family made up of sons and daughters in His likeness, the God likeness or nature.[20]

> Praise be to the God and Father of our Lord
> Jesus Christ, who has blessed us in the heav-
> enly realms with every spiritual blessing in
> Christ. For He chose us in Him before the
> creation of the world to be holy and blame-
> less in His sight. In love He predestined us to
> be adopted to be His sons through Jesus
> Christ, in accordance with His pleasure and
> will. To the praise of His glorious grace,
> which He has freely given us in the One He
> loves. (Ephesians 1:3-6 *NIV*)

Before the creation of our world, Christ was already committed to the plan and the will of God concerning the redemption of mankind. God purposed that none should perish but that all should come to repentance.[21] Therefore all mankind is predestined according to *Ephesians 1:3-6*, to become the sons of the living God. God's word says that "Jesus Christ had shed His blood not only once, but also for all." Another way for us to look at what Christ was saying would be to say that all mankind has been forgiven of their sins. Each individual must accept the forgiving power of God, or the sacrifice that brought forth forgiveness would remain powerless within their individual lives. Here's an illustration to support the forgiveness of all sin, through the death and resurrection of Jesus Christ.

If I held a million dollars in my hand and at the same time offered it to all mankind as the only solution for poverty, those who chose to receive the money would empower themselves to walk free from their present condition. The money is offered to all, though each individual must ask for the power to break the back of poverty within their own life. This is the same principle concerning salvation and the forgiveness of sins.

"All sins are forgiven, though not all mankind asks to receive forgiveness."

We learned within the first chapter a godly principle concerning first the natural then the spiritual. It's vital to gain a good understanding of this principle in order to relate natural fatherhood to spiritual fatherhood. As we begin in this chapter, we'll first deal with the family structure concerning fathers in the natural and then continue progressing toward the family structure of God concerning the need for spiritual fathers within the body of Christ. "*Why fatherhood?*" is a question that we must first answer and then deal with, in order to lay a strong foundation in which the rest of this book will be established.

Family Structure in Today's Society

We are starting to see the overall effects of single parents through their children as a direct result of divorce. Tragically divorce is considered to be a permanent solution to what is really a temporal problem. It has the appearance of resolve but in reality produces a greater problem, "*dysfunctional families*", and the inability to function according to true biblical pattern. There may very well be at times scriptural grounds for divorce, though the dysfunctional order, which is contradictory to God's biblical pattern, still remains.[22] A functional family consisting of a male and female, must first be represented through the covenant of marriage, in which both individuals join together in the witnesses of others and vow to honor, love and cherish one another till death do them part. The only way the institution of marriage can progress into a family is through the conception and birthing of offspring or through the adoption of children. The emphasis is placed on the fact that both parents must be present within the family structure. "Whether adopted or not, in order for a marriage to become a family, there must be the presence of children."

When building a natural house "material structure," the most important step is to be sure to lay a solid foundation on which the rest of the structure can be built according to the structural order. Without a solid foundation and strong structural form, the house would be considered dysfunctional to the proper pattern that was established within the original blueprints. This is a picture of the same principle that relates to establishing the institution of marriage. Both a solid foundation and structural order must be established within a marriage between a husband and wife before the rest of the house can properly be built.[23] We all know that a house is not a home until you actually move in and add all the personal touches. Well, this is also the same principle within the family structure. A marriage consisting of a solid foundation and structural order is not a family until there has become the indwelling of offspring whether natural or adopted.

Mothers Were Never Called To Be Fathers

Let's take a brief look at the functional role of a mother in the natural family structure and the effects of her responsibilities within the lives of her children. We need to understand first that mothers operate in a completely different function than fathers. Mothers within the natural family carry the function of *"loving"*, *"nurturing"*, *"teaching"*, *"and imparting of wisdom"* and *"establishing within the heart of the children the necessity for affection."*[24] Mothers seem to be more protective over their children at times than fathers, and also seem to have more difficulty letting go. I understand that what I'm sharing with you is nothing new to the understanding of most men and women today. Though the importance of reiterating these functions of motherhood will prove vital once we start to parallel the functional role of a natural mother with the responsibilities of a spiritual mother.

The hardest question to answer as a single mother or

father is *"How do I fulfill both functional roles of parenthood in order to see that my children never do without?"* So many times we've seen single mothers trying to operate in their God-given function of motherhood, though at the same time trying to fulfill the functional role of the father as well. This is an impossible task that will quickly drain the life and willpower right out of you. As single Christian mothers, we need to gain an understanding that the only true replacement for the absent father, *"that you are required to fulfill"* is to become double the mom. As you become the entire mom that you can possibly be, you must then allow the release of your children into the hands of the Holy Spirit and trust that He will bring the God result concerning fatherhood in their lives.

The tragedy lies in the fact that most single parents do the exact opposite. With a strong desire for raising their children, they try to fulfill the functional role of both a father and mother, though the end results are children who will lack both the motherly and fatherly characteristics.

Responsibilities of Fathers

Just like mothers, fathers walk as well in a specific function, with many specific responsibilities. A father's responsibility is first and foremost to his family, in which he is responsible for providing safety, security, stability and provision. One of the greatest responsibilities that a father has been given by God, in regards to raising his children, are both discipline and instruction. Unlike the motherly characteristics, the father seems to be geared toward stricter discipline; this is necessary within the lives of the children in order to develop strong character and identity.[25] Fathers, carry the responsibility of imparting long lasting characteristics and values to their children that will empower them to boldly walk out and fulfill their destiny in life.[26] It's vital concerning the full development of all children, for the strong influence of a father *"whether natural or stepfather,"* to be present within their lives. God holds fathers as well as mothers accountable for the "training", "teaching" and "instruction" of their children.[27]

> Train up a child in the way he shall go, and
> when he is old he will not depart.
> (Proverbs 2:6 *NIV*)

Fathers are responsible for speaking destiny into the lives of their children and seeing that identity is formed within their hearts and minds.[28] To speak **destiny**, means *to reveal within the heart of each child, a predetermined course for living.* Speaking destiny instills vision, as well as prepares an inheritance for each child. Keep in mind that a father has never been given a mandate by God to control his children's destiny. A father must continue to build up and encourage his sons and daughters in order to help direct and fashion that which God Himself has purposed for each child. The key to fashioning true identity is through right relationship communicated from the heart of the father to his children. **Identity** means *the condition of being oneself, not being conformed to another.* As fathers we need to understand that our children have their own identities; we must assist in bringing out the best in them so that they'll gain an understanding of who they are. Mothers, as well, function in such a way that helps shape and direct the lives of their children, although the ultimate responsibility rest upon the shoulders of the father.

Spiritual Family

It's important that we become familiar with the functional role and responsibilities of both the mother and the father within the natural family structure. Just as there are fathers in the natural family, there are also fathers within the spiritual family. Before we begin to discuss spiritual fathers, it's important to take some time and first introduce the structural order of the spiritual family or spiritual house.

All through scripture we're taught *"first the natural and then the spiritual"* (*1 Corinthians 15:45-49*). This is the same principle on which a spiritual family or spiritual house is built. Just as in the natural family or natural house, above all else *"**Father God**"* is the head, Even though many natural families deny the existence of God or His Son Jesus Christ. The truth remains; He is still Lord and supreme authority over all things. Second in the structure of natural family or natural house would be the *"**father**"* of the household. According to the word of God in Genesis, the husband shall rule as the head only second to Christ.[29] Then we see that the *"**mother**"* would become the next level of authority, as the *"**children**"* would complete the structural order of the natural family.

Based upon what we have just discussed concerning the structural order of the natural family, it's important that we understand that the natural family parallels with the same structural order on which the spiritual family or spiritual house should be governed. *"**Father God**"*, who is the head of all things, once again is supreme authority over the spiritual family or house. Second only to God is the gift of God, *"**spiritual father**."* A spiritual father *"whether male or female"* that has been set by Christ over a spiritual house, is one who holds functional office as a five-fold ministry gift.[30] Spiritual fathers are delegated representatives of Father God, given as gifts to the body of Christ. The functional role of a spiritual father is to unite the body of Christ through first laying and then establishing within the hearts of men and women an inheritance of God's true pattern for biblical living.

Third following after the function and responsibilities of a spiritual father, we have within the spiritual house, responsibilities of the *"**spiritual mother**."* A spiritual mother is not a title with a functional responsibility of only one particular person. The role of a spiritual mother within the spiritual family is not a functional office or an appointed function. The fulfillment of a spiritual mother is the responsibilities that are shared throughout the entire body, within the spiritual family or house. The result of the body of Christ actively walking out the responsibilities of the spiritual mother is discipleship.

Ultimately the entire body is called to operate within the responsibilities of the spiritual mother. We as the body should continue to build one another up in the most holy of faith, through loving, nurturing, teaching, imparting wisdom and continually showing each other the need for affection. As we have learned, these are also the responsibilities of the natural mother, within the natural family or household.

Responsible for role as spiritual father
(Governing Elders)

1. Apostles
2. Prophets
3. Evangelists
4. Pastors
5. Teachers

Responsible for role as spiritual mother

1. General Elders
2. Deacons
3. Spiritual Sons

Responsibilities of a Spiritual Mother

The general elders, deacons, and spiritual sons joined and jointed to the vision of God, within the spiritual father are responsible and held accountable for operating within the responsibilities of the spiritual mother.[31] General elders, deacons, and spiritual sons must begin to understand their God-given responsibilities within the spiritual family, and then each one must actively begin to administrate the responsibilities of the spiritual mother one to another. Therefore the spiritual family is made complete, through the functional role and responsibilities of a spiritual father and through the responsibilities of the general elders, deacons, and spiritual sons portraying the spiritual mother through discipling one another within the spiritual family or house. Thus the spiritual family is now functional, with the present responsibilities of both the spiritual father and spiritual mother.

We can't allow ourselves to become caught up with gender; it's important that we gain the understanding concerning the functional roles and responsibilities that need to be displayed within the body of Christ. Without the responsibilities of the motherly characteristics, the body of Christ would continually be raised as a dysfunctional body (family). Remember that if only one parent is left with the responsibility of raising his or her children alone, then that family is considered dysfunctional, ,which means the family is now operating outside the original structural order or pattern.

The title, "spiritual mother" because of the female gender or even responsibilities placed upon general elders, deacons and spiritual sons, may cause a lot of red flags to go off right here in the beginning of the book. I'd ask that you allow the material the ability to be presented with an open heart and mind. God is presently restoring His Church back to the responsibilities and structural order of the spiritual mother. Remember that the responsibilities of a spiritual mother rest upon the shoulders of all spiritual sons who have gained an understanding of the God vision within the spiritual father. As well as all general elders and deacons appointed by God within the local family structure "spiritual house."

"Church as we've known it is changing, God is bringing His people out of limited thinking, in order to bring them into the realms of endless possibilities in Christ Jesus."

Why Spiritual Fathers

The gift of God "spiritual father" has the responsibility to raise, equip and then release the sons of God to do the work of ministry. This is accomplished through teaching and imparting the true structure of God's Divine Order and Godly Government.[32] We will cover both God's Divine Order and Godly Government in full detail in chapter six, although I would like to give a brief introduction that will help us lay a foundation concerning both.

God's Divine Order deals with aligning oneself up with biblical patterns and principles. Not according to the patterns and principles of man "Taught only for self elevation." Rather it is the leading of the Holy Spirit for the purpose of elevating Christ. God's divine structural order for the existence of mankind is the fact that we are spirit, we have a soul, and we live in a body. Most people within church as we've known it have been taught to operate outside of godly order through aligning oneself up with the patterns and principles of man, which state that we are body, soul, and then spirit. This concept focuses totally on the natural realm and denies believers the correct understanding concerning how to live according to the spirit of life, instead of living bound by sin and death. Divine order can only be established within the hearts of men and women of God, as long as we make the willful choice to deny our fleshly desires and pick up our cross and follow after Christ "Spirit led Spirit Directed."

Godly Government is essentially family, family structured, and family based. Church, as we've known it, continues to operate outside of the godly structural order of family. When the Church stops being the family of God, we become nothing more then just another organization in which we attend simply out of tradition. The promises of God rest within His Government, though until the body comes in line with God's Divine Order, the Church will remain living in lack concerning promises that are made available through Godly Government.

Remember the statement that was made concerning the fact that the functional role of the natural father was to speak the destiny of his children? Well the same is true for spiritual fathers. Let's distinguish the difference between the responsibilities of the spiritual mother and the functional role of the spiritual father.

Many of us that are reading this book have had wonderful people lead us to the Lord. Individuals that *loved* and *nurtured* you and were very *protective* over you, toward the fact of wanting nothing to hinder the work that was being established within your heart and life. They were probably *teaching* you the principles of God's word, as well as walking the full term with you, while you were presently in the birth canal waiting to emerge as a true son of God. It's also possible that they celebrated the victory with you concerning your new life. Allow us to ask you a question, *"Where are they today?"* The answer to this question will help define the difference in functional roles concerning the spiritual father and the responsibilities of the spiritual mother.

It could be that you rarely ever see or hear from them. There is even a stronger possibility that after you received Christ, you decided too never look back and the very one that led you to the Lord, you've now surpassed through a maturity in the faith. These individuals would not be considered spiritual fathers, though in a sense they did mentor you or instruct you for a season in the faith. The underlined words above are actually the functional role of the natural mother, as well as the responsibilities of the spiritual mother.

> I have been reminded of your sincere faith
> which first lived in your grand mother Lois
> and in your mother Eunice and I am
> persuaded now lives in you.(2 Timothy 1:5-6
> *NIV*)

We can see from this passage of scripture that both Lois and Eunice played a vital role in the life of Timothy. Apostle Paul clearly states that it was the love of Timothy's grandmother and mother that actually birthed Timothy into the Kingdom of God. It would be safe to say that both Lois and Eunice sired Timothy into the kingdom of God.

> I write these things not to shame you but as
> my beloved sons to warn you. For though
> you have ten thousand instructors in Christ,
> yet not many fathers. For in Christ Jesus I
> have begot you in the gospel. (1 Corinthians
> 4:14-15 *NIV*)

There is clearly a distinction between instructors, tutors, and mentors in the word of God. Although all of the above operate within different responsibilities of a spiritual father concerning the progression of all believers, though none of the above completely fulfill the functional role of a spiritual father. Paul the Apostle speaks of having begot his sons through the gospel, to **begot** means: "*to be the father,*" "*to cause produce as an effect.*" Paul was saying that he was willing to accept the responsibility for producing the life of Christ in others according to the gospel. Fatherhood is more then just introducing an individual into the kingdom of God; it's literally reproducing the Christ nature "*Character*" in the lives of God's sons through raising, equipping and then releasing spiritual sons into their destiny, for works of service unto the Lord.

We are all familiar with the process of conception concerning the natural birth of a child. As we all know the male stores up seed, which is the power to bring forth life and upon intercourse transfers the seed of life to the womb of a woman. Now the conception in the natural can take place. I know this seems elementary, though lets look at the spiritual implications for a moment. Just as the male is needed to sow natural seed within the female in order to produce life, we as the bride of Christ, need to spend time alone with Father God, so that in these times of intimacy, His word (seed) can be sown into our hearts.[33] As the seed of Christ penetrates our hearts, then we become empowered to sow that very seed into the lives of others and continue to produce the sons of God in the earth.

Remember that God's governmental structure is *family*. We will learn in chapter six that the Government of God is essentially family, family structured, and family based. So as the bride of Christ, we must operate in our functional role and responsibilities as the female and *"become fruitful and multiply,"* This can only happen, when we come into intimacy with the father, and allow His seed "Word" to be sown into our hearts. It takes the union of both Father God and the bride of Christ, in order to become fruitful and multiply. If we can grab a hold of what the Holy Spirit is trying to reveal to His Church, we will never walk in complacency again, as well, we will begin to see a greater need for intimacy with Father God.

Spiritual fathers are responsible for reproducing the Christ nature within the hearts of the sons of God, which are entrusted to them by God. As we start to gain understanding of the functional role in which a spiritual father operates, we will began seeing a pattern concerning spiritual fathers leading their spiritual sons into God-given identity, through directing them toward their destiny in Christ. It's vital that we see right here in the beginning the enormous amount of responsibility that God has placed upon the shoulders of a spiritual father.

Governing Elders and General Elders, Same Qualifications different Responsibilities.

Here is a trustworthy saying: If anyone sets his heart on being an overseer, he desires a noble task. Now the overseer must be above reproach, the husband of but one wife, temperate, self controlled, respectable, hospitable, able to teach, not given to drunkenness, not violent but gentle, not quarrelsome, not a lover of money. He must manage his own family well and see that his children obey him with proper respect. (If anyone does not know how to manage his own family, how can he take care of God's church?) He must not be a recent convert, or he may become conceited and fall under the same judgment as the devil. He must also have a good reputation with outsiders, so that he will not fall into disgrace and into the devil's trap. (1Timothy 3:1-7 *NIV*)

It's important for us to gain the understanding that there are two types of elders, *Governing Elders* and *General Elders*. *Governing Elders* are God's delegated representatives to the body of Christ; they are apostles, prophets, evangelists, pastors or teachers. *General Elders* are men and women that share the same qualifications as a governing elder though their function of responsibility is different in the spiritual house. General elders are both recognized and appointed as spiritual overseers by the governing elder's "*spiritual fathers*" in the spiritual house. Keep in mind that governing elders do not have the ability to appoint whomever they chose as general elders within the spiritual house. As governing elders *"spiritual fathers"* begin to establish a relationship and direct the spiritual sons through God-given instruction toward their destiny; then God will reveal to the spiritual father or fathers those whom He has designated to assist in overseeing spiritual matters within the spiritual house.

Not all-general elders **"men and women that qualify for eldership,** are appointed and set by God to function in the office of an apostle, prophet, evangelist, pastor or teacher, *1 Timothy 3:1-7.*", Though general elders still posses the qualities to be recognized by Father God, as spiritual leaders within a spiritual house. General elders oversee, maintain and resolve spiritual matters in the spiritual house, as well as assist God's delegated representative "spiritual father" in teaching, training, instructing, and imparting destiny and identity, into those God has placed within the spiritual house.

It's important to understand the need for strong relationship between the *governing* and *general elders*, relationships established through accountability and responsibility one to another. Through right relationship, general elders must always have the right to speak into the lives of all governing elders "Five Fold Ministers", whether it is for *conformation, affirmation, correction, instruction or rebuke*. Even though general elders have the ability to speak into the governing elders lives through right relationship, never gives the general elders the right to try and control and manipulate God's governing elders *"spiritual fathers"*, though through right relationship, general elders must have a voice.

"Governing elders are also general elders though not all general elders will become governing elders"

True Deacons and their Qualifications as well as Responsibilities in the Spiritual Family "House"

> In those days when the number of disciples
> was increasing, the Grecian Jews among
> them complained against the Hebraic Jews
> because their widows were being over
> looked in the daily distribution of food. So
> the Twelve gathered all the disciples together
> and said, "It would not be right for us to
> neglect the ministry of the word of God in
> order to wait on tables. Brothers, choose
> seven men from among you who are known
> to be full of the spirit and wisdom. We will
> turn this responsibility over to them and will
> give our attention to prayer and the ministry
> of the word." This proposal pleased the
> whole group. They chose Stephen, a man full
> of faith and of the Holy Spirit; also Philip,
> Procorus, Nicanor, Timon, Parmenas, and
> Nicolas from Antioch, a convert to Judaism.
> They presented these men to the Apostles,
> who prayed and laid their hands on them. So
> the word of God spread. The number of
> disciples in Jerusalem increased rapidly, and
> a large number of priests became obedient to
> the faith. (Acts 6:1-8 *NIV*)

Deacons are not intended to be held responsible for overseeing spiritual matters within a spiritual house "Family"; though in order to become a deacon you must be full of the Spirit of God and walk in His wisdom *1 Timothy 3:8-13*. Deacons assist the general elders by concerning themselves with the natural responsibilities on a daily basis within the spiritual house concerning God's people. The functional role of a deacon allows both the governing and general elders the ability to freely attend to spiritual matters that otherwise would not properly be attended to, if they were spending the majority of their time dealing with natural matters among God's people.

Remember the biblical principle that we established within chapter one "Kingdom Principles" first the natural then the spiritual. True deacons, "Godly men and women qualified for natural service" contribute a large part to the success and advancement of the vision of God. True deacons allow the governing and general elders the ability to operate unhindered within their God-given function, to ensure the full success of God's vision for the spiritual family as well as all generations to come.

Spiritual Sons

Spiritual Sons are male and female; Men and women that have gained and is living daily with the revelation that they are the true church of Christ Jesus instead of walking with the understanding that they are just attending church. In order for one to become a spiritual son, one must dedicate his or her life through submission to the message as well as godly vision that God Himself has placed within the heart of the spiritual father, "*Five-Fold Minister, Governing Elder, God's Delegated Representative or Representatives.*" A spiritual father or fathers have been called appointed and set by God over the spiritual house or family. God joins spiritual sons to spiritual fathers based on the destiny and calling of the spiritual son.

Spiritual sons are birthed out of right heart-shared relationship with Father God. As the sons of God start to desire all that God has for their lives, then God will speak to their hearts as to where and when He wills to establish a solid foundation of Christ, revealing destiny and building identity within each son of God. We must understand right here in the beginning that spiritual fathers never go looking for spiritual sons, though the heart of a true spiritual father must continually be open to receive God's sons. It is the responsibility of both men and women of God, to join themselves through the unction of the Holy Spirit, to a spiritual father or fathers.

Spiritual sons are those men and women of God that have committed their entire life to the call of Christ. Spiritual sons are men and women who have committed their lives to the fulfilling of their destiny in Christ. Spiritual sons are prepared to submit to the authority of Christ within others in order to be taught, trained, instructed, equipped, corrected, or rebuked if necessary and released into the work of ministry and the destiny that God established for each and everyone before the foundations of the world. Spiritual sons are not afraid of change nor do they feel intimidated submitting to the Christ nature within the spiritual father.

"Spiritual sons are the key to patriarchal succession, generational blessings and the continual establishing as well as revealing within the hearts of both men and women, an eternal inheritance in Christ, that will forever exist from generation to generation until the end of time."

Children
To this point we have discussed the functional role of the mother and father within the natural family. We have discussed the responsibilities of a spiritual mother and introduced the spiritual father within a spiritual family. We have also discussed the qualifications and different responsibilities between governing elders, general elder and deacons as well as introduced and explained to some detail spiritual sons within the spiritual house or family. Next, we need to discuss the children within the spiritual family, which parallel with the children in the natural family.

Understand that all believers are saints *"Governing*

elders, General elders, Deacons, Spiritual sons, Children."
Saints represent individuals that have been sanctified or set
apart in Christ Jesus through acknowledging Christ as Lord
and Savior.[34] Spiritual fathers *"governing elders"* and spiritual sons are saints, as well as general elders and deacons.
Though as saints, they have gained the understanding of
their responsibilities within the body of Christ, responsibilities that cause them to mature and increase in knowledge
and understanding, concerning their destiny, identity, and
calling in Christ in order to advance the Kingdom of God.

Just as in the natural family, there are also children
present within the spiritual family "house." The saints
which fail to ever increase in knowledge and understanding
as well as those saints that have been active in ministry for
years though have never joined and jointed themselves to
God's delegated representative " *Spiritual father*" represent
the children within the spiritual family "house." The majority of saints within church as we know it are classified as
children based upon their lack of willingness to accept
responsibilities within the spiritual house. The majority of
children are those saints that are attending church instead of
gaining the understanding that they are the church of Christ
Jesus. Church buildings all over the world are filled with
born again men and women "Saints" that really have no
vision or direction concerning God's will and ways for their
lives or the lives of others.

The mindset of children has always been to receive,
though never willing to give. Church as we've known it
continues to quote the phrase *"We are just sinners saved by
grace."* The truth is that once we receive Christ as Lord and
Savior, we are no longer sinners but saints. Therefore we are
saints saved by grace. God has not only called us to have the
knowledge of being born again "Saints", but to mature into
His sons manifesting His glory within the earth. Scripture is
very clear concerning the importance of saints, although in

today's society we've seemed to lose the true definition of what it means to become a saint of God.

Know this: we're not called to live only as saints, but to live as sons of God. As long as we continue to walk with the mentality that "I am just a saint of God saved by grace", then we as the body of Christ will continue to remain powerless over the influence of the enemy.

Safe Guard against False Spiritual Fathers

Jesus said to the crowds and to his disciples: The teachers of the law and the Pharisees sit in Moses' seat so you must obey them and do every thing that they tell you. But do not do what they do, for they do not practice what they preach. They tie up heavy loads and put them on men's shoulders but they themselves are not willing to lift a finger to move them. Everything they do is done for men to see. (Matthew 23:1-5 *NIV*)

But you are not to be called rabbi for you have only one master and you are all brothers. *Do not call any one father, for you have only one father and he is in heaven.* Nor are you to be called teacher, for you have one teacher the Christ. The greatest among you will be your servant. For whoever exalts himself will be humbled, and whoever humbles himself will be exalted. Woe to you, teachers of the law and Pharisees, you hypocrites! You shut the Kingdom of heaven in men's faces. You yourselves do not enter, nor will you let those enter who are trying to. (Matthew 23:8-13 *NIV*)

Jesus was speaking to the multitude as well as teaching His disciples. He was instructing them not to make deities of men but to exalt and lift up only the name of Christ. A spiritual father is God's delegated representative given to help develop and establish within the hearts of men and women, intimate relationship with Father God. The spiritual father is a functional office ordained by Father God, not an appointed title or position set by men. As sons, we must never allow the spiritual father to take the place of our relationship with Father God. Nor must we ever place a spiritual father above Father God.

This is the perfect opportunity to speak briefly about the wonderful truth that'll safeguard men and women against false spiritual fathers. False spiritual fathers are those who are looking only to control and manipulate God's sons for personal power and self-elevation. It's important to understand that a son must hear clearly from God that he or she is called to join to a particular spiritual father. One of the qualifications of spiritual fathers must be to have a deep cry within the heart for spiritual sons, and the heart must continually burn for the establishing of God's kingdom: "Righteousness, Joy, Peace" within the heart of men and women.[35]

Spiritual fathers must have expectancy within their hearts towards receiving spiritual sons. Once the "father-son relationship" has been established, the spiritual fathers will take on the responsibility of raising and releasing spiritual sons into the hands of God for service. We must understand that as spiritual sons, we first and foremost belong to God and God only, the spiritual father is only a natural picture that relates to our Heavenly Father. False fathers will arise to try and elevate their status within many religious circles, though from gaining the understanding within this book, you'll be well prepared to recognize them.

False Fathers are men and women who have denied the godly influence and personal accountability of others to ensure the safety of the sons they are raising and the message they are imparting. False Fathers lack true accountability, in outside relationship with other men and women of God; they seem to believe that all they need is a relationship with God the Father.

The truth is that a relationship with Father God is the first and most important line of relationship and communication needed for fathers to grow and mature, as well as impart biblical truths into the lives of their sons. Though if we deny both ourselves and the sons we are raising, the ability to be held accountable by the relationships of others, then not only the spiritual father but the whole spiritual house is in danger of walking in heresy based upon their own personal revelation. As Spiritual Fathers, we should always remain teachable, even to the place of being taught by the Spiritual Sons that God has entrusted to us. What better line of accountability then to trust and be willing to listen to the very ones you have sown your entire life into?

As Spiritual Fathers, we can not afford to remain an island to ourselves. We must gain an understanding that true Fatherhood depends on and even exists through our relationships with others and the ability to allow others to speak into our lives concerning the direction in which we're heading at any time. True Spiritual Fathers should never be intimidated by the influence or even correction of another, if their true heart is to see godly sons raised and the Kingdom of God extended within the earth.

Within this chapter it's possible your theological thinking may have been stretched, though I know that the parallel from the natural family to the spiritual family has been clearly portrayed. We must start to put the tools in which God has entrusted us to work in order to see the Church of Jesus Christ awake out of her slumber. Without recognizing and then applying the pattern of spiritual family structure, then we as the body of Christ will continually walk around the same mountain over and over again, never allowing ourselves to enter into the promise land.

"Church as we've known it must change, and the only way church as we've known it will change, is when leadership as we've known it changes."

CHAPTER THREE

Hannah's Cry

Have you ever had a desire that burned within your heart, so strong that all your thoughts were consumed in one direction? I'm sure it's safe to say that at one time or another we have all felt this way about something or someone. The fact that we have all been touched in some way or another by this type of experience will allow us to enter into this next chapter and begin to draw from the revelatory truths through the power of the Holy Spirit. I'd like for you to meet someone who's very special to me and we know that she will grow very dear to your hearts as well. I'd like you to meet Hannah. Please understand that Hannah has been through quite a bit over the years, although she has truly seen the hand of the Lord move mightily on her behalf. I thought it would be best if Hannah herself shared with you all that have taken place within her life.

As you have already been told, my name is Hannah. I would like to start by saying that it's a privilege to share with you the goodness of God within my life. I am the wife of Elkannah, though I am only one of two wives within our family, Elkannah's other wife is named Peninnah. As I think back, why don't I start by sharing with you a little about myself? I guess you would say that I am the type of person that can get along with everyone that I meet; though some would say that I am a bit reserved. I can honestly say that I don't believe that I have ever met a stranger. There seems to be this love and compassion on the inside of me that always challenges me to reach out and hug the unhugable and love the unlovely.

Well, unlike those of you who are reading this book, I was born and raised with the understanding according to the Law of Moses. Therefore upright and blameless living was represented by the acts or deeds of obedience according to the Law that governed God's people. One of the most sacred acts that I would perform was the fact that once a year the whole family was expected to offer up sacrificial offering for the cleansing of sins, these offering would consist of sacrificing animals. I know that the sacrificing of animals seems quite messy for someone who lives in the 21ˢᵗ century to even consider, though this form of sacrifice was as normal to us as lifting your hands and dancing before the Lord is to you.

In my family there has been many children born, although none of which has come from my womb. You see it had appeared for a time that the Lord in his sovereignty allowed my womb to remain barren. For this reason my husband Elkannah who loved me very much, would always give me a double portion of meat when we as a family would go up to the house of the Lord to offer our sacrifices. In return of his kindness, I thanked the Lord daily for him; I know that it was God that gave him to me. I believe that it was my responsibility to love, honor, and cherish him all the days of my life, just as it was his responsibility to treat me with the same respect.

As the years went on my barren state continued and I

had started to grow somewhat bitter in soul. The inner most parts of my being were continually crying out for a son. Time and time again my womb would continue to deny the power that was needed to carry the sown seed. Please understand that this was as well a time of great irritation, the fact was that Peninnah "Elkannah's second wife" seemed to find great joy in my pain. She seemed to enjoy provoking me to that place of irritation, as she would constantly remind me that a woman that could not produce offspring was a curse. Every one knew that the words of God unto all mankind was "Be fruitful and multiple." So you can understand how I felt, a woman that loved God though lacked the power to help fulfill his plan for mankind.

Year after year Peninnah would always say the same hurtful words that seemed to leave wounds that would never heal. I can remember one time in particular when as a family we had gone to the house of the Lord, in order to bring our yearly sacrifices. Peninnah was continually reminding and provoking me concerning my barren state. I had become so grieved that I could not even eat. I can remember my husband trying to comfort me with as much compassion as he knew how. I can still hear the questions that he asked.

> "Hannah, why are you not eating?"
> "Why are you weeping?"
> "Hannah, why are you down hearted?"
> "Don't I mean more to you then ten sons?"

As loving as he knew how, he tried to solve the problem with only a few simple words, although the healing process was more than he could have ever imagined. What he had failed to see was the fact that a husband is not capable of fulfilling the place of a son.

Though still bitter in soul after speaking to Elkannah, I

then began to cry out to the only one that could turn my mourning to dancing again. As I began to lift up my prayers before the Lord, I was in such deep anguish and distress that the desperate cry of my prayer had bypassed my mouth and was coming straight out of my heart! As I cried out I said "Lord my God, if only you will give me a son I will then give him back to you for the service of ministry all the days of his life?" "Father if you would so choose to release the deadness of my womb and allow life to come forth, I would willfully establish covenant with you on behalf of my son." You see that which I was asking was for the Lord to honor my son with the nazarite vow, which is a vow of separation unto the Lord. What I had asked was for God to perform a sovereign work on the behalf of the son I so much wanted to conceive, carry and then give birth to. While still praying I was disturbed by "Eli" the High Priest of the day.

"How long will you continue to keep getting drunk, get rid of your wine?"

You could imagine my surprise when I heard him speak. "Not so my Lord, I am a woman that is deeply troubled, I have not been drinking wine, I was pouring out my soul to the Lord. Please do not take your servant for a wicked woman, I have been praying out of my great anguish and grief." At that moment "Eli" this seemingly old and lifeless man of God rose up and began to speak a word so bold that I could do nothing else but believe it. Eli said "Go in peace and may the God of Israel grant you what you have asked Him!" At that moment I knew that the Lord had, not only heard my prayer but also answered it as well.

The next morning I can remember the excitement as my husband called me into the bedchambers to lie with him. You see the Lord had remembered me that day, for my womb, which was once dead, had now been recreated and made alive. For the first time I bore a son and called him Samuel; saying "Because I asked the Lord for him." He was all I could have ever hoped for, the very apple of my eye! I can remember continually asking myself the same question over and over again,

"How could it be possible to create someone so lovely that words can not even express?"

I can honestly tell you the truth that I have never seen one so radiant and full of joy, he was truly a beauty to behold. Though never losing sight of the vow I made with the Lord, I continually offered up praises to my God for the great things He had done.

Once again it had become that time of year in which we as a family would present our sacrifices. Knowing the task that laid ahead of me, I asked Elkannah for permission to stay and honor my covenant with the Lord concerning Samuel. With a deep understanding of covenant, Elkannah was willing to allow me to take the necessary time to properly wean Samuel. Once Samuel was weaned, I would then have to release him into the hands of the Lord whom he would serve for the rest of his life.

Finally the day came in which Samuel would be presented to Eli "High Priest" in order to serve within the house of the Lord forever. As we left along with Samuel, Elkannah and I brought a "three-year-old bull," "Ephah of flour," and a "Skin of wine." After we had slaughtered the bull, then we brought our one and only son to Eli the priest. As I approached Eli, I began to explain to him that I was the woman that had stood before him in prayer a number of years ago. I remember the exact words that I had spoken to Eli.

"I prayed for a son and the Lord has granted me that which I have asked Him, and now I am to release him in order for him to minister to the Lord for the rest of his life."

As a mother there was no way I could continually stay away from my first born, and I knew that it would have not been the will of God for me to do so. So once a year, I would

visit Samuel and bring him a linen ephod, which represented priesthood. This was my way of continually speaking
destiny into his life, just as I had the day that I prayed and
asked God for the right to have Samuel serve Him all the
days of his life.

I want to be as real with you as I know how; it was not
an easy thing to do, giving up my only son. The truth is that
not a day went by after the birth of Samuel that I had not
entertained thoughts of keeping my child. The one thing that
kept me straight was the fact that I knew the blessing of the
Lord rested within obedience. As sure as the Lord destroyed
the power of death and then brought forth life within my
womb, could he not create for me another son!

Without going into much detail, Peninnah who was at
first "Fruitful and Multiplied" has now, what we call
"Pined away." She had now become very sick, which caused
her to grow barren and now lacks the ability to bare children. Though born unto me including Samuel, God granted
seven children. We all know that seven represents the
number of God.

**"The Lord brings death and makes alive, He brings
down to the grave and raises up."**

I want to thank you for the opportunity to speak today
and I hope my testimony will prove vital for your progression in life.

It's important that we gain an understanding concerning
the life of Hannah. There are not a lot of scripture concerning Hannah to expand on so we must take the little we have
and place our trust in the Holy Spirit to bring forth the revelation. Though I have conveyed my overall look at the life of
Hannah according to the scriptures that we've been given, I
trust that you will not take my word as the complete gospel.

Therefore you should research and validate all that is spoken within this chapter as well as the whole book.

Hannah's Characteristic Traits of a Spiritual Father

Hannah, like a tutor or an instructor seems to have portrayed many of the characteristic traits of a spiritual father, though it would not be correct to say that she is a complete picture of a spiritual father. I'd like to point out three different functions of a spiritual father that Hannah displayed through the time of her life before and after she gave birth to Samuel. Hopefully this will allow us to continue laying a strong foundation for spiritual fathers. I would ask that you allow your heart and mind to remain open in order to gain understanding concerning God's revelation to His Church.

First Characteristic Trait —Desire

Through the Biblical accounts of Hannah's life, we have learned that she had a strong desire to raise a family.[36] Remember that marriage is not a family until there has either been the procreation of offspring or the adoption of children. It's important that we see and understand that "Hannah's cry" was for a son, one that would serve "*Minister to*" the Lord all the days of his life.[37] This is a very critical part of structure concerning spiritual fathers. There first must be within the heart of a spiritual father, the desire to receive sons. This strong desire must then develop into a cry from the heart of the father for sons.

> See I will send you the prophet Elijah before the great and dreadful day of the Lord comes, He will turn the hearts of the fathers to their children and the hearts of the children to their fathers; or else I will come and strike the land with a curse. (Malachi 4:5-6 *NIV*)

We are all familiar with the pictures in the Old Testament where the mothers always seemed to be the ones who cried out for their sons.[38] We've also seen the picture quite clear to the fact that mothers had a strong desire to conceive and then give birth to children.[39] Many men feel as though these are only the characteristics of the female gender. Remember that we are neither male nor female within the eyes of the Lord. The old covenant, which was natural law, has passed away and the new covenant, which is the law of spirit, now abides. I don't believe that it's a coincidence so close to the new covenant being established that this scripture concerning *God "turning the hearts of the fathers to their children"* was recorded.[40] God was establishing a new order, which is the order of His Spirit. It's imperative that we gain an understanding concerning the fact that God's divine order for daily living is *"spirit, soul, and then body."*

Unless God turns the hearts of the fathers toward the sons, it's impossible for true sons of God to be born. Natural man must cry out to God with the desire to see the hearts of men and women changed and through their desire, just as with Hannah, God will meet their cry. [41]

It's not to say that men and women within ministry whose hearts have not yet been turned to receive God's sons lack the ability to raise sons, though they lack the ability to raise the sons of God, *"true godly offspring."* Outside of God's true structural pattern, men and women within ministerial circles will continue to reproduce the sons of man, as long as their hearts have not been turned toward spiritual fatherhood. In most cases, the reproducing of ministerial sons within the structure of church as we've known it; has had the appearance of godly sons though they've lacked the character and godly understanding to function properly within the structure of the spiritual family.

"As long as we are walking within the Governments

of man, then we are incapable of operating within the order of God."

Remember that the Government of God is essentially family, family structured, and family based. As the body of Christ, we are called to live under the governmental structure of "**Theocracy**" which means: *a form of Government in which a deity is recognized as the supreme ruler.* As the Church of Jesus Christ, we should allow Christ to remain supreme ruler over our ministerial exercises and all that it entails.[42] Though church as we've known it continues to operate within the structure of "**Democracy**" which means *a Government in which supreme power is exercised directly by the people or their direct agents.* Democracy is a form of man- made Government. Just as many nations have different governmental structures, God has His Governmental structure and its family. God never planned for the body of Christ to gather for celebration and equipping of the sons of God, within the man made structure of Democracy.

Can you imagine where the natural family would be today if it were run under the governmental structure of Democracy? Allow me to give you an example. Would you take a vote within the household to see who would drive the car to the store, knowing that not every one within the household is old enough to drive? Though this sounds quite silly, we need to understand that this is how church as we've known it is presently being run. It appears that everything must be voted on and the saddest part is the fact that we have taken all spiritual authority away from the minister and have placed it upon the shoulders of the deacons. Deacons were never called to control spiritual matters within the spiritual family.[43] Man's structural pattern of Church as we've known it, allows the congregation along with the deacons to choose their spiritual guidance *"minister"*, and if for some reason we don't agree with the message which challenges us to raise our standard of living, then we simply fire the messenger.

"For the sake of future generations, we can't afford to continue to build upon this man made foundation of sinking sand!"

Jesus said "*I will build my Church and the gates of hell will not prevail.*"[44] So why does it seem like the gates of hell are prevailing over the Church? The reason is that church as we've known it is operating outside of true godly structural order. Through the hearts of men and women, God is presently restoring His Church back to Divine Order and Godly Government. We must have an ear to hear and a heart to respond to the true structural order concerning the spiritual family and the functional roles of each and every member within the family. Only as long as the hearts of the fathers are turned to the sons and the hearts of the sons are turned to the fathers, then that which is restored within this generation will continue within the next.

The spiritual father must have the same characteristic trait as Hannah (Desire) to see the sons of God "birthed" "raised" and then "released" to minister unto the lord all the days of their lives. Once the father's heart has been turned by the Holy Spirit to receive sons, then the Holy Spirit will begin to turn the hearts of the children to receive fathers. It will take a strong effort on both the fathers and sons in order for that which God has restored in this generation, to continue throughout the next.

Second Characteristic Trait —Speaking Destiny

We see in 1 Samuel 1:11 the ability of Hannah to speak destiny into the life of her unborn son. The fact that he was "*unborn*" is a very important keyword for fathers today. After the desperate cry from within Hannah's heart for the ability to receive a child, she then through prayer began to speak that which wasn't as though it was. She asked the Lord concerning the vow of separation for her son, as if Samuel were already born.[45] She was speaking destiny within the life of Samuel concerning his service of ministry unto the Lord. As fathers and those that will become fathers we need to grasp this simple but profound truth. *"From the abundance of the heart the mouth speaks,"* therefore as our hearts begin to turn towards sons, we should then start to speak forth the existence of sons.

I am not in any way establishing a formula for building large congregations, with the understanding of church, as we've known it. We have never been given a mandate to build church. We do, on the other hand, have a mandate to build a *"Holy Nation."*[46] What is being presented within this book is the true godly pattern for building and advancing the Kingdom of God.

Let's talk about the importance of Hannah visiting her son once a year and then bringing him a linen ephod. We see that after the birth of her son, Hannah continued to speak destiny into Samuel's life, through making Samuel a linen ephod *"garment of covering."*[47] The ephod represented priesthood, so you can see that in a small but very profound way, Hannah helped direct her son into his God-given destiny while at the same time helped him establish identity. It's important to understand that the responsibility rests upon the fathers to speak and direct their sons into God-given destiny much like we have seen and learned from Hannah.[48] Hannah was communicating through the linen ephod that her son wore that Samuel was royalty, a son of the king *"son of God."*

Let's take a look at the meaning of destiny; destiny *is a predetermined course of events.* All mankind has a predestined plan to become the sons of God. God's main *"Purpose"* *"Plan"* and *"Design"*, as Father God is to establish godly bone structure within the sons of God.

He predestined us to be adopted as His sons
through Jesus Christ, in accordance with His
pleasure and will. (Ephesians 1:5 *NIV*)

As we have seen, God's purpose is family and multiplication of godly offspring. If this were a pattern that God
Himself through Christ continues to establish from the Old
Testament to the New, then why would we think God's
structure would be any different today? We must begin
building family instead of organization. There is only one
pattern or structure that we must follow and that is the
pattern and structural order of God. As we begin to allow
the Holy Spirit to reveal God's truth concerning family
structure then we will also start to see the desperate need for
fathers within the body of Christ.

Fathers must operate within two specific functions in
order to speak forth destiny and begin to direct the sons into
their God-given identity. The first function is through declaration. The second function is through administration, apostles and prophets work together to declare and administrate
God's word, for the establishing of godly principles and
structure. A father may not be a prophet or an apostle
concerning functional office, though he or she must still
function in the areas of declaration and administration, in
order to speak destiny and direct his or her sons toward their
God-given identity. It's important to remember that even
fathers are first and foremost sons of God.[49] As sons they
carry the ability through the Holy Spirit to be used as He
wills.[50] So if God has called you to become a father, then
He will also empower you to operate within the functional
roles of declaration and administration.

Declaration

As fathers our functional role of responsibilities will
only be accomplished if we have developed first for

ourselves an ear to clearly hear what the Spirit of God is saying concerning His sons.[51] You see God's plans are endless for the sons that He's entrusted to a father. True fathers must see the sons through the eyes of God, or else the destiny of the sons would be limited.

Remember in God's structural order of family, the father carries the responsibility and functional role for sowing *"establishing"* destiny and identity into the hearts of the sons. This is not a pattern or structure established by man. This is God's way of communicating His blueprint for godly living within earthen vessels. Here is one of the questions that is most asked within religious circles.

"Are there not successful men and women of God within the structural order of Church as we've known it?"

Yes, though they've been recognized solely based upon their gifting and anointing, lost within the confines of historical church, lay apostles and prophets, evangelists and preachers, as well as teachers. Men and women of God with a heart for the truth; though denied the understanding of their true calling in Christ, because of the lack of fathers, within church as we've known it. So we have apostles walking as pastors appointed by man and prophets trying to fulfill the functional role of an evangelist, because of their boldness and zeal. We've made teachers intercessors and evangelist's a one-man circus, individuals who must perform every time he or she is in town.

"How can these mighty men and women of God though never growing up within the structural order of spiritual family, walk in the power, anointing and gifting of God?"

The gifts of God and His anointing are automatic within the life of all believers.[52] Just because some draw on both the anointing and the gifting more than others, doesn't mean that one believer has more of God's anointing or gifting then another. The truth is that the anointing and the gifting will never qualify a man or woman for ministry. In order to become a man or woman of God you must be zealous, though it takes more than zeal alone to become a son of God; it takes relationship. Relationship must never be birthed out of ministry, though ministry must always be the direct result, birthed out of relationships. It is not the anointing or gifting of God that will establish one's ministry, though it is the relationships birthed out of his or her spiritual family that will not only establish but also launch sons into their God-given destiny and calling in Christ.

Once God's plan, purpose, and intent is made known to the fathers as well as the sons, then the fathers have the responsibility to bring forth godly direction and instruction concerning the lives of God's sons. The reason that declaration is vital to the lives of all sons is because that which is spoken should never become the words of man but only the words of God, from the heart of Father God. The spoken word is considered seed, therefore, once the word is sown or planted within the hearts of men and women then that seed now has the power to germinate or grow. So if you sow the God seed, then you will surly reap the God harvest. The problem in church as we've known it is the fact that we've mostly sown the seeds of man; therefore we have only reaped the harvest of man. We don't know about you, but were more then ready to reap the God harvest. We must awake out of the slumber of religion and remove the veil that we have placed over our heads. We must begin to function within the ministry of Christ Jesus,[53] manifesting the Kingdom of God within the earth, continually pushing toward the ultimate goal of reconciliation established through relationship one with another.

> Then God said let the land produce vegeta-
> tion seed bearing plants and trees on the land
> that bear fruit with seed in it, according to
> their various kinds and it was so. The land
> produced vegetation; plants bearing seed
> according to their kind.
> (Genesis 1:11-12 *NIV*)

We can't afford to misunderstand the parallel between
the natural and spiritual work concerning the principle of
sowing and reaping, as well as seed and harvest time. Jesus
said, *"The kingdom of heaven is like a mustard seed, which
a man took and planted in his field."* It's vital to the progression of the Kingdom of God that we as fathers continually
plant the God seed in order to reap the God harvest within
the lives of the sons of God that have been entrusted to us.

Administration

Now that we have seen the need for sowing the word of
God, which is *"seed"*, into the lives of the sons, we must
begin to see the importance of watering God's seed in order
for growth to take place within their hearts. We understand
the simple principle concerning the natural, which states the
fact that, "We must water a seed while in the ground in
order to cause that seed to produce the fruit within."[54] This
natural principle of watering is paralleled with the spiritual
principle of watering. *"Through administration, the word of
God begins to grow within the heart of men and women."*
Administration is the process in which the seed of God's
word receives water in order for growth to take place.
Watering the seed of God consists of equipping the
sons through *"Teaching" "Instructing "Directing"* and
"Imparting" God's Divine Order and Godly Government

through right relationship that is established upon unconditional love.

I know this seems like an overwhelming amount of
responsibility that is being placed upon the shoulders of the
fathers, though God is faithful to meet the needs of those
who desire true godly structure and the multiplication of
God's word into the lives of others. As sons of Father God,
we have the ability to operate within all that is needed to
raise the sons of God that will be entrusted unto us. The
only requirement is that we must first allow God's Spirit to
lead us *"Spirit directed"* and have a willing and obedient
heart to respond to the call of God for our lives. Aside from
God, we lack the power to turn our hearts toward the children, though when God turns our hearts, then we'll have all
the power that's needed to manifest the kingdom of God
within the lives of the sons through the Holy Spirit.

We see all throughout the Gospels how Jesus not only
declared the word of God concerning destiny and identity
into the lives of His spiritual sons (Disciples) though He
also brought an administration to the spoken word as well.
Keep in mind that you will not father every son of God
"member of the spiritual house", only those who have
joined themselves to you by the unction of the Holy Spirit.
We find in scripture that Jesus always ministered to the
multitude, although He taught the disciples "sons"
(Matthew 5:1-2). As fathers you will always be required to
minister to the multitude, though with the understanding
that you are only raising and equipping the sons.

Fathers must allow the Holy Spirit to properly teach us
how to administrate the declared word that we have spoken
over God's sons, in order to see the seed of God grow to
maturity. Administration applied to declaration is just like
adding water to a natural seed, "it's necessary in order to
bring forth life."

Third Characteristic Trait —Weaning

The third and final characteristic trait of Hannah, which can be related to the characteristic trait of a father, is the function of weaning the sons of God or releasing them to do the work of ministry. Hannah understood from the beginning that though giving birth to Samuel, he was still not hers to keep. Hannah knew that Samuel was only required to stay with her for a time and a season. Samuel was only allowed to stay within the comfort and protection of his mother while she was fulfilling her functional role through nurturing Samuel to a place of weaning. It's very important to hear what the Holy Spirit is saying at this particular moment.

Samuel's maturing would now bring his release for ministry unto the Lord. It's vital for the maturity of spiritual sons that fathers gain revelation through what is being imparted throughout this segment. Sons are entrusted to fathers for a time and season. There will come a time when the majority of the sons must be released to function as either spiritual fathers in their own house *"Spiritual Family,"* or joining with other men and women of God to unite vision. Not all-spiritual sons will become spiritual fathers though all sons must be released in order for them to fulfill God's plan for their lives. Many sons will be released into ministry though may never leave the spiritual house. Through the ministry of Jesus, we find the true pattern for fatherhood concerning the responsibilities of raising, equipping, and then releasing the sons of God to do the work of ministry.[55]

Upon the conception and then birthing of sons, the responsibility for development now rests upon the shoulders of the father. The father alone lacks the ability to bring the sons to full maturity. Many different functions and characteristic traits are needed to mold and shape the sons of God. This is why we're one body though with many different functions and members. It takes a collective effort on the part of the entire spiritual family to bring a son to full development, though the father is held responsible for the direction and instruction that leads to the maturity or weaning of the sons.

We have been taught in some circles that the word of God is both meat and milk. Though how do we make a distinction between which scripture is meat and which scripture is milk? The whole word of God is the milk, which allows our body to grow and mature. So if the word of God is milk, then what would the meat be? The meat is within the manifestation of the word *"Faith with out works is dead"* *"Faith comes by hearing and hearing by the word of God."* So if faith is through the hearing of the word, and we are to be rooted and grounded in the word then the word must be a necessary form of life in order to grow and mature. The word of God births faith within the hearts of all believers; therefore God's word is vital for new believers in order to allow the birthing process to progress men and women into maturity.

The action or works of our faith would be considered the meat that causes the body to grow to full maturity. Once a son comes to the place of maturity after partaking of the milk, he/she must then be released and given the opportunity within the spiritual house to eat of the meat, which is the responsibility of manifesting that which he or she has been taught.

Milk nurtures a child and allows him or her to start growing and maturing. The very thing that is needed to bring stability and growth in the infant stages will eventually bring death if that's all the child eats. There must come a time when we partake of solid food for strength and stamina. The solid food of the gospel is within the manifestation of the teachings we have already learned and gained a solid understanding of. The milk is the whole word of God, brought forth through *"Teaching"* *"Instruction"* *"Directing"* *"Studying"* and *"Meditating"* upon the Holy Scripture.

CHAPTER FOUR

Eli's Sons of Unrestraint

Have you ever felt as though there weren't enough hours within a day to complete all the tasks that were needed? As men and women presently confined to this world, we seem to be powerfully dominated and ruled by the pressures of time. Time unfortunately seems to govern our ability to operate within a day-to-day basis. Though sad, the truth is that each and every day must be scheduled just right in order to accommodate time. While we continue to live as a product of our environment "enslaved to time," there will always be valuable aspects that unfortunately never receive attention. The fact is the majority of our time is focused toward daily agendas that are designed to examine and resolve material matters. There is a downside to the way in which we spend our time. Though daily many of our material needs are accomplished, mankind still continues to suffer from lack of inter-relationships one to another.

Relationships are the key that will unlock the hearts of man. Without relationships communicated one to another then we as flesh and blood begin to walk within the function and characteristics of a mechanical machine. A machine is incapable of sharing or expressing emotions, while at the same time has no understanding or ability to function with moral and ethical values. Also a machine is not concerned with anything else that is going on around it. These characteristics of a mechanical machine seem to demonstrate a shocking parallel to mankind within our world today.

In this chapter we'll be dealing in detail concerning our desperate need for relationships one to another, and also the effects, as a direct result of the lack of relationships within church as we've known it. We'll use Eli and his sons Hophni and Phinehas in order to convey the outcome caused by lack of relationships. You will also see the danger within the lack of relationship between a spiritual father and his or her spiritual sons, as well as the dramatic effects it'll have on other people.

Hophni and Phinehas

First and foremost, we must understand that Eli's sons were considered wicked men, men that had no regard for the things of God. The word *"wicked"* as stated in the original writings is *"**Belial**"* which means, *"worthless wicked men, destroyers, prince of evil."* In later years the word Belial was properly used concerning the name and character of satan.

"How could this be, didn't Eli "The Priest" raise Samuel within the house of the Lord and Samuel turn out just fine?"

As we progress we'll see the outcome of Samuel and his sons as a direct result through being raised by Eli as his spiritual father (*1 Samuel 2:12*). "They knew not the Lord." The word *"knew"* speaks of a form of relationship established through intimacy one with another. We can see this pattern of intimacy within the institution of marriage between a husband and wife. It's important to understand that both Hophni and Phinehas lacked an intimate one-on-one relationship with their heavenly Father. Relationship is our most important key as believers.

"Lack of relationship causes lack of identity, lack of identity causes lack of discipline, and through lack of discipline is birthed "sons of unrestraint."

Let's once again take a brief look at the meaning for "*identity.*" Identity means the condition of being oneself and not another. We need to understand that identity is established through relationships one with another. Though the pressure of life surrounds us, we cannot afford to allow time to suffocate the ability to develop inner-relationships one with another. Men and women of God need to gain the understanding that without the ability to establish true lasting relationships, then all that God has restored in this generation; will die in the next. As we look at the lives of both Hopni and Phinehas as a pattern concerning the lack of relationship with God, we'll also discuss the lack of relationship between their natural father "Eli."

Hophni and Phinehas Denied God

> Now it was the practice of the priest with the people that when anyone offered a sacrifice and while the meat was being boiled the servant of the priest would come with a three-prong fork in his hand. He would plunge it into the pan or kettle or caldron or pot and the priest would take for himself, whatever the fork brought up. (1 Samuel 2:13-14 *NIV*)

Hophni and Phinehas were truly wicked and vile men, though they walked as priests of their day. The sons of Eli were robbing the people of the ability to give all that they were required to sacrifice as an offering. They were so wicked within their hearts that they literally had no fear of God whatsoever! It would be safe to say that neither Hophni nor Phinehas had the slightest recollection of reverence for the things of God. They were driven by their own lustful passions and both had become lovers of themselves and not lovers of God. Not only were they attempting to make a mockery out of God through robbing the people of their offerings, they were also defiling and corrupting the women of God by lying with those who served at the entrance of the tent of meetings. They were willfully prostituting or playing the harlot with the church "*God's people*" for self-gratification and personal gain. How does Hophni and Phinehas relate to ministers within church, as we've known it? Today, many men and women of God walk with the same mentality as Eli's sons of unrestraint, *"As long as you need me "**The Minister**" you can please me!"*

"Did Hophni and Phinehas grow up within the house of Eli the High Priest?"

"Did they not eat as children before the table of Eli?"

"Did they not sit under Eli's ministry while growing up?"

The answers to all of these questions are more than likely yes. So why did they turn out as sons of unrestraint? Both Hophni and Phinehas lacked one-on-one relationship with their natural father, and through their lack of natural relationship, they'd never learned how to effectively establish a relationship with Father God. If a child is trained "taught" to walk in the reverent fear of God, through learning how to establish the right relationship when he or she is younger, then when they are old, they will not depart.

Train up a child in the ways he should go and
when he is old he will not depart.
(Proverbs 22:6 *NIV*)

God's People Playing the Harlot

As long as the body of Christ continues to cry out *"Please give us your seed, so we can feel good"* with no intentions of reproducing the sown seed, then we too, are found guilty of prostitution. We play the harlot with God's delegated representatives *"Five-Fold Ministers."*

Prostitutes have no desire or intentions to carry the sown seed. They have no vested interest in the enormous amount of responsibility it takes to care and nurture the seed in order to bring forth a harvest. Many of God's people are playing the Harlot, seeking only after the revelation and manifestation of God for self-gratification, with no desire to reproduce or reap a God harvest. We must stop seeking and worshipping the manifestations of God, *"Gold dust, Splitting pulpits, Holy laughter, Slain in the Spirit, as well as Spiritual goose bumps."* We must start to seek an intimate relationship with Father God through worship. Worship should be an outward expression of our intimate relationship with Father God, a true evaluation of who God is.

Within this segment, I'm not intending to pass judgment upon God's people or His Priesthood, though desiring to provoke the hearts and minds of both men and women within church, as we've known it, to change. We must come to the place where we allow Christ to unite His body through covenant relationships, so that the true Church can start to reproduce after its own kind *"Christ."* Without biblical covenant relationships related and practiced throughout the entire body of Christ *"You and I"*, then all the revelation that has been revealed within this generation will become nothing more then wasted seed.

"There must once again be a desire and longing for a line of righteousness brought forth through correction and instruction back to the Church, You and I."

Eli the Priest

God had not only called but also appointed Eli as High Priest over all Israel. So Eli was actually responsible for God's house therefore he was held accountable for those in which he was placed in authority over. So what happened within this man of God that allowed a gap to form between himself and both his sons, "Hopni and Phinehas?" Could it have possibly been that fact that Eli, though called by God into ministry, became so driven and consumed with the work of ministry, that he forgot the most important ministry that God had given him, *"The ministry of raising his children?"* You see we always tend to look at the sons as the problem, when in fact they were just an outward manifestation of an inward problem. The problem lay with Eli and his lack of ability to develop a one-on-one relationship with his sons.

You see that it's so easy to pass judgment on the younger generation, for the condition of the world in many nations. The youth have never been the problem just the manifestation of the problem. We must always remember that youth will continue to function as youth, just as children will continue to function as children. We as natural fathers and mothers must take on the God-given responsibility of properly raising our children within the reverent fear of God. We must establish individual relationships with our children. So you see, individual relationships must first and foremost be taught within the natural family structure. How else will our children ever understand how to establish a relationship with Father God, if there has never been a solid foundation of relationship laid for them to build upon?

The character of love should first be instilled into the heart of the child through the care and compassion of both the natural father and mother within the family, followed by the members within the family structure. It's important to understand that the responsibility rests upon the shoulders of both the father and the mother, who function in God-given authority over their sons and daughters.

Many men and women still have a problem with understanding and receiving the love of God within their lives, even though they are believers. This is a direct result of the overwhelming lack of direction and instruction, followed by not receiving genuine love within their natural family as children. As parents it's vital for the growth and development of our children that we instill the necessity for love. Remember that one of the functions of a mother is to instill within the hearts of her sons and daughters the necessity for affection and love. As we learn to receive the love of Father God as parents who lacked the opportunity to receive love while growing up, we'll now carry the capability of instilling true godly love into the hearts of our children. Understand that this is the same pattern for a spiritual family concerning the establishing and teaching the need for love through right relationship, into the hearts of the spiritual sons.

Let's talk about the condition of Eli concerning the later years of his ministry and at the same time relate his condition, to the condition of church as we've known it. The word of God says, "Eli had *"grown old"* and *"obese"*, while at the same time was *"losing his eye sight."*

> One night Eli's eyes were becoming so weak
> that he could barely see, he was lying down
> in his usual place. (1 Samuel 3:2 *NIV*)

We see according to this scripture that Eli the High Priest of Israel was not only growing old but he was also losing his eyesight. Let's look at this picture of Eli and his physical condition with spiritual eyes, while at the same time keeping an open heart and mind to the revelation within God's word.

Could it be possible that Eli had not only lack relationship with his sons as a direct result of his God-given ministry, though through time had developed a lack of intimate relationship with Father God? According to the word, we should place nothing above Christ "*Christ should be exalted*, **Not Ministry**." As men and women of God, we must make sure that nothing comes between our relationships with Christ. Ministry is the work of Christ, not "*the Christ*."

Many that are reading this book are totally consumed with the work of ministry to the point that your family suffers the consequence of your actions. It's time to stop and reevaluate who God is and what His reason for calling you into His ministry was in the first place. Church as we've known it will continue to walk outside of God's Divine Order as long as we continually deny the Government of God "*Family Structure*" within the body. Before we are called to minister to the nations, we are first called to minister to our natural family.

It's very possible for ministry to become an idol within the lives of men and women of God. You see we can become so consumed or caught up with worshipping the move of God that we forget to worship the one who moved, "**Father God**."

We read within God's word that Eli's eyes had become weak; Eli was losing the vision of God. The heart that once burned for the truth and direction of God for future generations had now become weak and complacent. Eli is an Old Testament picture of ministries today, operating outside of New Testament Patterns and principles. Many men and women of God have lacked the ability to establish a long lasting intimate relationship with Father God; as a result many have lost the vision of God. As we look at the natural picture of Eli's condition, and relate it to ministries in today's society, we'll begin to see an explanation for the lack of godly sons within the universal church?

Let's look at another aspect of the passage, "Eli was lying down in his usual place." This is a very interesting piece of scripture if we parallel it with the condition of church, as we've known it. With the vision of Eli now growing dim, he would continue to function within the old patterns that were most comfortable to him. You see, without vision, Eli was only capable of operating within the old structure or thought patterns of what he'd already known. Therefore Eli was forced because of his lack of vision to become complacent and settled in all his ways, to the point of just existing. The plan of God for our lives has never been to just exist. God's plan was never for His church to lose vision. Loss of vision leads to complacency and becoming settled in "*our*" ways. Christ was made flesh so that you and I would have the ability to extend the vision of God through multiplying godly offspring within the earth through the power of the Holy Spirit.

We can also parallel the fact that Eli had become obese within the natural, to the condition of Church, as we've known it today. As the body of Christ, we have two options once we've heard or received God's word within our hearts. We can consume the seed "*God's Word*" and become obese, which will deny the power of the sown seed to procreate spiritual life on the inside of others. Or we can sow God's seed "Word" into the hearts of men and women throughout our world, in order to multiply the Christ nature within the nations. A true spiritual father always sows the God seed into the lives of his/her spiritual sons, in order for both the father and the sons to reap the God harvest.

Rebuke Not Received

Now Eli was very old and heard about everything his sons were doing to all Israel and how they slept with the women who served at the entrance at the tent of meetings. So he said to them, why do you do such things? I hear from all the people these wicked deeds of yours. No my sons it is not a good report that I hear spreading among the Lord's people. If a man sin against another man God may mediate for him; But if a man sins against the Lord who will intercede for him? His sons however did not listen to their fathers rebuke, for it was the Lord's will to put them to death. (1 Samuel 2:22-25 *NIV*)

"Through lack of relationship we're denied the true ability of speaking into an individual life."

So you see; this was the case concerning Hopni and Phinehas. Even though Eli was their natural father, he still had the responsibility of raising his sons through an individual relationship in order to rightfully gain the ability to speak into their lives. The fact that Eli was told of the acts or deeds that his sons had been performing for a long while, shows that Eli had denied both of his sons a personal relationship with their father. If Eli had walked in relationship with both his sons, he would have known the condition of their heart. Eli's relationship with his sons would have afforded him the God opportunity to speak into their lives and administrate godly change. Remember that a natural father must raise and instruct his sons and daughters through establishing right relationship in order to speak into their destiny.

Fathers must function within the characteristic traits of both correction and instruction. If fathers function without correction or instruction toward their children while establishing an individual relationship, then father God will hold them accountable. Without God, it's impossible to correct the rebellion that exists within young adults, as a result of the lack of individual relationship. So as parents we must first earn the respect of our children by setting an example, by establishing individual relationships with each child, in order to gain the right to speak into their lives. We have all gained the basic understanding concerning the fact that *"Respect must be earned and not demanded,"* so why do we think this principle would be any less different concerning our children? Natural and spiritual children are both gifts entrusted to us by God; we are only the stewards of God's gift.

As we come in line with the true structural pattern of God, then we will see the nations healed, although the healing process must first start with one family at a time.

Eli's Consequence For Lack of True Fatherhood

> For I told him that I would judge his family forever for the sins he knew about; his sons made themselves contemptible, and he had failed to restrain them. Therefore I swore to the house of Eli the guilt of Eli's house will never be atoned for by sacrifices or offerings. (1 Samuel 3:13-14 *NIV*)

Judgment had now fallen on the house of Eli because of his inability to establish the right relationship with his sons. Remember that only through relationship has an individual gained the right to speak into the life of another. We also see the effects of the lack of relationship between Eli and his sons. The Priesthood of Israel, which was God's established order within the house of Eli's father, had now been striped away (*1 Samuel 2:30*). The Lord speaks concerning His previous order with the house of Eli, *"Far be it from me, those who honor me I will honor, those who despise me will be disdained."* **Disdain** means *to think unworthy of notice.* So we see that through the inability for Eli to restrain his sons the Lord changed His order of Priesthood within Eli's lineage forever.

The Judgement of Eli

> The time is coming when I will cut short your strength and the strength of your father's house so that there will not be an old man in your family line, and you will see distress in my dwelling. Although good will be done to Israel, in your family line there will never be an old man. Every one of you that I don't cut off from me will be spared only to blind your eyes with tears and to grieve your heart, and all your descendants will die in the prime of their life.(1 Samuel 2:31-33 *NIV*)

As you can see, Eli was held accountable for the actions of his sons. No longer would the wisdom of the older generation flow from the line of Eli's lineage. We see that Eli's lack of stewardship, not only affected his immediate family, but also the lives of all those who were yet to be born. The Lord said that his descendants would all pass away within the prime of their lives. This may seem quite harsh, although we must understand that when we've been entrusted with a gift from God, he expects us to become the best stewards we can. Remember our children belong to God and he has only entrusted them to us so that we can raise and equip them to the best of our ability through Christ as good stewards of God's gift. Eli is the perfect example of a father that wasn't a good steward of the gifts that God had entrusted to him.

"Men and women of God, as your hearts are turned toward the sons of God. I charge you in the name of Christ,

to raise the sons that are entrusted to you with all the ability God has given, through demonstrating God's love and establishing individual relationships."

As spiritual fathers, you will be held accountable for the raising of God's sons. It's important that we learn from Eli and his sons the patterns of what not to do. If we lack the ability to manage our household, then how will we ever be able to take care of the House of God? We must understand that the house of God is not a physical building, but a live and vibrant body of Christ, built up into a spiritual house made out of living stones.

Samuel Ushers In the New Order

According to what we've learned within chapter three "Hannah's Cry," Hannah had given her only son over to the house of the Lord to minister all the days of his life. The word **minister** means *to serve as a menial "Domestic servant"* or *"Worshiper."* Just as we've also previously learned, God honored the vow of separation, which Hannah had prayed for with by her cry of desperation for a child. As we'll see, God honored her pray in the most honorable way, by establishing His new order through Samuel. That, which was taken away from Eli because of his inability to restrain his sons, was re-established within Samuel.

> The Lord said to Samuel see I am about to do something in Israel that will make the ears of everyone that hears it tingle. (1 Samuel 3:11 *NIV*)

> The Lord was with Samuel as he grew up and He let none of his words fall to the ground, and all Israel from Dan to Beersheba recognized that Samuel was attested as a Prophet of the

Lord. The Lord continued to appear at Shiloh
and there He revealed Himself to Samuel
through His word. (1 Samuel 3:19-21 *NIV*)

Samuel grew in the Lord, and as a seal of his functional
office, not a word that he spoke fell to the ground. So we see
that the very words that were spoken through the mouth of
Samuel were accurate and always came to pass. God had
now established His word within the life of Samuel and thus
a Prophet was born. Samuel walked as a mighty man of
God, sold out entirely to God and the work of ministry.
During the early life of Samuel he was always found sleep-
ing by the ark of God. This represents the fact that Samuel
was found to always be within the presence of God. Only
through exposing himself to God's presence was he able to
hear the voice of the Lord. As men and women of God it's
vital that we follow this same pattern and continually
remain in the presence of God regardless of where we are or
what we are doing. As long as we're Christ-centered and not
self-centered, then we'll always have an ear to hear what the
spirit is saying. We must continue to become spirit lead and
spirit directed (*Romans 8:14*).

Samuel's Sons

It's very interesting when we read concerning the
outcome of Samuel's sons. Would you believe they turned
out just like Eli's sons? Once again there is little scripture to
establish a solid foundation concerning the reason for the
lack of restraint within the sons of Samuel. Samuel had
become a product of his environment. Samuel reproduced
the same seed that was sown into his life through Eli his
spiritual father, "*Seed of ministry.*"

It's important to remember that Samuel's mother continued to speak destiny into her son every year. We have
learned that she would always bring him a linen ephod,

which speaks of priesthood. Samuel never turned out as Eli's natural sons, because Samuel continually had destiny spoken in and over his life. As well, he was not only called but also appointed by God to functional office. God chose Samuel to walk in priesthood.

As we're talking about the character of the sown seed of Eli into the life of Samuel, we must then understand that every seed produces after its own kind. If you plant an apple seed it will produce an apple tree that will in due season yield apples. The same with a watermelon seed, it'll produce and yield watermelons. Another way of looking at this picture is to say, "If you plant "**ministry**," you will produce ministry." We must stop sowing only seeds of ministry, and start to sow seeds of God's Divine Order and Godly Government concerning spiritual family. According to the pattern that we've established within this chapter concerning the lack of relationship between Eli and his sons, Samuel had learned through Eli, that ministry was more important than his family. Keep in mind that we were never called to raise God's sons to look like us "spiritual father." God's sons must only bear the image and likeness of Christ, though the spiritual father is responsible for equipping the sons with the Christ seed.

> Samuel continued as judge over Israel all the days of his life, from year to year he went on a circuit from bethel to Gilgal to Mizpah, judging Israel in all those places. But he always went back to Ramah where his home was, and there he also judged Israel, and he built an altar there to the Lord. (1 Samuel 7:15-17 *NIV*)

> When Samuel grew old he appointed his sons as judges for Israel, the name of his first born

was Joel and the name of his second was
Abijah and they served at Beersheba. But his
sons did not walk in his ways. They turned
aside to dishonest gain and accepted bribes
and perverted justice. (1 Samuel 8:1-3 *NIV*)

As tragic as it may seem, Samuel followed right into his
spiritual father's footsteps. Though Samuel was an obedient
servant of God and his words never fell to the ground, he
like Eli was denied the power, "*because of lack of relationship with his sons*" to reproduce godly offspring. The last
section of this chapter will deal with three types of relationships that are needed in order to bring balance into our spiritual and natural lives.

Father Relationships

The first level of relationship is between Father God and
His sons "*You and I.*" Within this level of relationship we're
taught that all men and women as believers must first and
foremost submit their lives to the authority of Christ. You
see, outside of any other relationship, there is none more
important than our walk with God. Once we've established
an intimate relationship with Father God, then we must
allow God to place us within fertile soil in order for us to
grow. So first we submit to God and only second to God is
our submission to our spiritual father and to the Christ
nature that lives within his or her heart. As we've discussed
earlier on in this book, God is first and foremost our Father,
though He has chosen to establish within man a natural
picture of our relationship with Him. So therefore it's vital
to the growth and maturity of the true sons of God that we
come under the leadership and authority of another.

We'll never walk in true God-given authority, until we
first learn to establish the level of relationship between
Father God and a spiritual father. Church as we've known it,

up until this point in history has been experiencing only the grace of God. Though as the Church of Christ Jesus, we need to move from solely operating by God's grace, into God's government, and then onto God's glory. Why is the church of today still operating solely by the grace of God? Church, as we've known it, since entering into the dark ages, has continually operated outside of God's Divine Order and Godly Government.

When we align ourselves up with God's true order, then we'll begin to move from grace into God's government, which is family. Then once we as the bride of Christ start to become the family of God, we'll begin to walk within His glory. God's glory means "God's manifested presence," as true sons of God we are called to manifest the presence or glory of God throughout the entire world.

What If My Minister Is Not a Spiritual Father?

The question most asked concerning this teaching. "What if I belong to a ministry in which the minister is not operating as a spiritual father according to *God's Divine Order and Godly Government?*" God alone knows where we need to be planted in order to grow to full maturity, the Holy Spirit will reveal to us if we're in the proper place of God's planting. The first thing we need to do is ask the Holy Spirit to reveal to us whether or not the minister to whom we've submitted, will allow his or her heart to be turned unto the children "Sons of God?"

We must take the material within this book and allow the Holy Spirit to begin to show us the true pattern for godly living. Understand that there are many men and women of God that simply haven't had the opportunity to hear such a message, so we need to remain patient and allow the Holy Spirit the opportunity to touch the hearts of both men and women. Men and women all over the world upon reading this book or hearing this message from another source will begin to leap within their spirits just as John the Baptist leaped within the womb of Elizabeth after the true message for mankind was spoken. If your minister is not operating with the understanding of spiritual fathers, there is still no ground to leave your local body, though it is grounds to ask the Holy Spirit if his or her heart would ever be turned toward God's sons. There is the possibility that your minister upon hearing the true structural pattern of God, will refuse to submit to the God plan and structure for God's Church; in this case, the Holy Spirit will lead you to a spiritual house functioning within true Divine Order and Godly Government.

"John the Baptist said "I must decrease and Christ must increase"

Peer Relationships

The second level of relationship that we as the true sons of God must walk within is the level of peer relationship. Peer relationship teaches individuals to walk in accountability with one another. Through accountability with one another, we as believers have the greatest safeguard for living as Christ. As long as we're walking in accountability with one another, then we won't have to worry about walking or heading down the wrong path. Accountability will always keep us in line with the plan of God for our lives. Also through accountability we begin to come in line with the word of God.

There are many times, we as believers, seem to become lost within the pressure and situations of this world. It's these times when we begin to really see the power of accountability. Though we may seem down, we're never out, as our peers began to speak words of life that immediately bring us back on track. We need peers/friends that are functioning on the same level and operating with most of the same understanding that we are. This will allow you and your peers the ability to communicate on common ground. We also need peers with different perspectives; this develops great depth within our relationships.

It should be those to whom you're accountable that will help you heal the hurts in your life, as well as bring deliverance to many situations. Remember the words of Jesus, after He commanded Lazarus to come forth. He was speaking to the disciple, "now *you go down, loose him and let him go*" (*John 11:41-44*). Before his death, Lazarus walked in accountability with the disciples. The disciples were his friend and therefore the very ones that were required to remove his grave cloths.

Church as we've known it seems to have the functional order of the minister all wrong. Ministers were never called to heal, deliver, and set the captives free within the God structure of Building His Church. The ministers are there to equip, teach, and basically act as a show and tell model for the sons to follow. We as the sons of God, held accountable to one another, are called to **"loose them and let them go."**

Disciple Relationships

We are all familiar with the great commission, *"Go into the world and make disciples of all nations."* The third level of relationship that's needed within the lives of every believer is the level of *"discipleship."* As we disciple one another, we then learn to walk in godly responsibilities. Remember that redemption wasn't the end of God's plan but the beginning. Whether we're called to become a spiritual father or not, we're all called to the ministry of discipleship, in order to advance the kingdom of God. We can all think back, concerning someone, "whether for a time or a season", that impacted our lives through discipleship. Those were the relationships, which really allow us as believers to know that someone truly cared.

We need to make sure that there is always someone

within our life that we assist, and bring to maturity with the gospel of Christ Jesus, through discipleship. Discipleship is not only necessary for the one whom you are helping to develop through Christ. You will be amazed at the spiritual growth that takes place on the inside of you, through becoming obedient by helping to establish and care for your brothers and sisters in Christ.

As we begin to disciple others we'll start to see the growth within our own spiritual life, we'll increase with knowledge and understanding of God's word. As we become faithful with the little, God will make us rulers of much. In this last half of the chapter, we have discussed the importance of relationship and how a lack of relationship will prove detrimental to the growth of an individual. It's vital that we gain an understanding concerning the three types of relationships that we as believers must continually walk in, in order to remain balanced and help ensure the ability to walk as the true sons of God.

CHAPTER FIVE

Who Are Called To Become Spiritual Fathers?

"Fathers raising sons is a biblical principle of responsibilities in relationship; the same principle as discipleship, where we are called to both accountability and responsibility. The father-son terminology indicates the depth intensity and sincerity of right relationship established in Christ for the sole purpose of advancing the Kingdom of God, throughout all generations to come."

"Who are called to become spiritual fathers?" This is one of the most valuable chapters within *"Fathering the Nations."* As men and women of God, we must first recognize and identify those who've been given a mandate or command by God to raise His sons. I'll once again ask you to open your spiritual eyes and ears in order to see and hear what the Holy Spirit is saying. There is a specific mandate given to men and women of God, in order to raise, equip and release God's sons into the work of ministry. In this chapter, we'll reveal the truths of God's word concerning spiritual fathers.

> But to each one of us grace has been given as
> Christ apportioned it. This is why it says;
> when He ascended on high, He led captives
> in His train and gave gifts to man. (Ephesians
> 4:7-8 *NIV*)

Upon the ascension of Jesus Christ, as He was called up and out of this natural world, the scripture says "*He gave gifts to man.*" The Church of Jesus Christ, "*The Holy City; The New Jerusalem*" has been given five ascension gifts by Christ Jesus "*Apostle, Prophet, Evangelist, Pastor and Teacher.*" These gifts that were given are an open show of God's *grace* to all those that remained in the earth, after the resurrection of Jesus Christ. There is plenty of material already out, "whether books or tapes" that wonderfully presents the message of God's grace. So with that said, let's briefly discuss God's grace manifested through the gifts that were dispersed to all mankind after the ascension of Jesus Christ.

God's grace represents "*God's power and ability made available to all that believe, even though we don't deserve it.*" God's gifts given to the church as a result of His grace must empower and equip all believers to function within the abilities of God "God-*Likeness.*" It's vital for the progression of the Church of Jesus Christ that we gain an understanding why we have been given these gifts from God. With this understanding we'll be able to properly recognize and identify who are called to be spiritual fathers.

> It was He who gave some to be Apostles
> some to be Prophets some to be Evangelists
> and some to be Pastors and Teachers. To
> prepare God's people for works of service so
> that the body of Christ may be built up until

we all reach unity in the faith and in the knowledge of the son of God, and become mature, attaining to the whole measure of the fullness of Christ.(Ephesians 4:11-13 *NIV*)

As we have seen through the above scriptures, Christ gave five different ascension gifts for the equipping of the body: Apostles, Prophets, Evangelists, Pastors, and Teachers. First of all, it's important that we understand that Christ is the "Chief" Apostle, Prophet, Evangelist, Pastor, and Teacher.[56] Therefore these gifts have been placed into the care of human hands by the grace of God *"His power and ability"*, and will only function properly through yielding ourselves to the leading of The Holy Spirit.

"It was never God's will to leave His sons fatherless, but to equip and raise His spiritual family with spiritual fathers."

A father to the fatherless, a defender of widows is God in His Holy dwelling. (Psalm 68:5 *NIV*)

Looking back to the first chapter *"Kingdom Principles"* we learned that we, "the bride of Christ" are *"Zion,"* the dwelling place of God in the spirit.[57] As the dwelling place of God, we must realize that it brought father God great pleasure to allow men and women the power and ability through grace, to be called the sons of God.

If you love me, you will obey what I command. And I will ask the Father, and He will give you another <u>Counselor to be with you forever.</u> — "<u>The Spirit of truth.</u>" The world can not accept Him, because it neither sees

> Him nor knows Him. But you know Him, for
> He lives with you and <u>will be in you.</u> I will
> not leave you as orphans; <u>I will come to you</u>.
> Before long the world will not see me
> anymore, but you will. Because I live, you
> also will live. (John 14:15-19 NIV)

Father God's purpose for sending His Son "Christ" to earth wrapped in flesh, was so that His creation *"You and I"*, would now have the power and ability to become one with our creator.[58] In demonstrating His love for all mankind, Father God's plan went beyond walking as mere flesh and reached farther then His willingness to shed His blood "God's Blood."[59] Even death and resurrection through the eyes of God, still wasn't enough to show forth His complete love and compassion as "Father God."

Aside from all the sacrifice for mankind, He continues to show forth His unconditional love through establishing in the hearts of all those who believe, His Son "Christ." *"I will not leave you as orphans; I will come to you."* Christ, the spirit of truth, is now our Counselor, that dwells in the hearts of all those who believe. Remember that the "Christ nature" or "likeness of God" was restored back unto all those who've received salvation, through the death and resurrection of Jesus Christ.[60] Therefore *"Not I that live, but Christ lives in me,"*[61] *"I am the Way, the Truth, and the Life,"*[62] *"In the beginning was the Word, the Word was with God, the Word was God,"* who was the word "Christ?" who is all these scripture speaking of *"Christ"* deity wrapped in flesh. [63]

As sons, we must understand, not only did God give His begotten Son in the beginning, He still continues to give Christ *"The Son of the living God"* today to those who believe. God is still giving all that He has, in order to see His sons grow to full maturity in the word "Christ." As fathers we must learn to understand God's love and begin walking as a show and tell model for God's sons that have been entrusted to us. Just as God gave His very life in the form of His Son "Christ," we as fathers are expected by Father God to give our very lives, in order to raise God's sons to maturity.

Just as we've seen throughout this whole book, concerning the principle of *"First the natural and then the spiritual,"* we'll once again need to use this principle while relating spiritual fathers to Father God. A spiritual father represents in the natural, a picture of our relationship with Father God. As visual people, we have been given through the grace of God a natural picture of God's love for His sons; this natural picture is the functional role of the spiritual father. Through the sovereign work of God, He has chosen to use human vessels, which have now become an extension of God's hand upon the earth.

God has entrusted five functional gifts to His Church "You and I", in order to raise and equip sons to do the work of ministry. The *"gifts of God"* that are entrusted unto His Church, are only five gifts out of the many fold characteristics of Christ. Though only five, God knew what gifts would be most needed in order to lay a solid foundation and establish the nature of Christ within the hearts of every believer.

Can Spiritual Sons Have More Then One Spiritual Father

God joins the heart of a spiritual father or fathers *"That has been set and appointed by Christ over a spiritual house, family"* to a spiritual son, by the unction and leading of The Holy Spirit. Once a father-son relationship has been established, the father or fathers now holds the responsibility for exposing the son to the remaining gifts of God.

Fathers and those who will become fathers need to understand that we alone through our functional office are not capable of properly raising the sons God has entrusted to us. It's important, in order for the complete raising of God's sons, that we understand God has given all five-fold gifts for the unifying of the body of Christ. Keep in mind that God's vision is not local or even within the confines of one particular nation. God's ultimate vision is *"Holy Nation."* He has given and entrusted all five-fold gifts for the unifying of His universal Church, "The sons of God." Therefore as a spiritual father, we're called to either the functional office of an apostle, prophet, evangelist, pastor or teacher, though there would still remain four functional offices needed to bring God's sons' "spiritual sons", to maturity. Therefore spiritual sons need the impartation of more then one-ascension gift "Spiritual father."

Each functional office is responsible for raising, equipping, and bringing spiritual sons to a place of releasing within their "functional ministry" specific gifting. Without the impartation of the remaining gifts, the sons that have been entrusted to the five-fold gifts "father or fathers" will lack the ability to grow to full maturity in Christ.

There's not one five-fold gift "functional office" that has been given a more specific mandate to raise, equip, and release God's sons "spiritual sons" to do the work of ministry. Each five-fold gift has been given a mandate to father spiritual sons, within the functional office that the spiritual father has been appointed and set by Christ to function within. If the functional offices of all five-fold gifts were present within a spiritual family *"Local House,"* then the spiritual family would be equipped with and be given by Christ, five spiritual fathers within the spiritual house. The ideal situation would be for all local houses *"Spiritual Families"* to be equipped with all five ascension gifts "Five-fold ministers." This would empower the sons of God "spiritual sons" with the ability to grow to full maturity in Christ Jesus.

The lack of all five ascension gifts within a spiritual house would not deny the spiritual fathers in the house from raising God's sons, though the spiritual family would become impaired, needing further impartation. For example, if an individual were to lose the use of his or her right eye, that individual would still function and utilize the left eye for vision. This individual "**though still with the capability to see**", would become impaired in sight. The loss of an eye would not render one useless, though would cause a slight disadvantage over one who has the use of both eyes. Those who are at a disadvantage must work extra hard in order to make up for their loss.

If two or more five-fold gifts were present within a spiritual family "House" each gift would submit to the functional office of the other. For example the spiritual house, in which I was trained and raised, has both the functional offices of an apostle and prophet present. When the apostolic office is ministering and functioning as the apostle over the spiritual house, the prophetic submits to the office of the apostolic that is made evident and manifested through "God's delegated representative." The same is true when the prophet ministers to the house by functional office. The apostolic submits to the prophetic office that is evident and being manifested through God's delegated representative. Gender makes no difference.

For example, think of one who tries to listen closely for the sound of a train in the distance, one who will listen with intensity to hear the cry of their own child, in a room full of children. What might you do to hear these sounds more clearly? Submit your remaining senses to the function most needed at the time, the ears. You would most likely close your eyes and focus on the sound you were trying to hear. Therefore just as the eyes would submit to the ears, so are God's ascension gifts given to His church, called to submit to Christ, "The *Word*" within each other.

Regardless of functional office, all five-fold gifts within a spiritual house must walk in accountability and submission to the Christ nature and mandate given to God's delegated representative or representatives, who have been set and appointed over the spiritual house by God. We must remember that we are not building our own kingdoms, rather the Kingdom of God. Therefore when we submit, our submission is unto the Lord and to the word He has spoken within our lives concerning our destiny and calling. God joins men and women to visionaries, men and women who will look past the four walls of church as we've known it and will say to God's people *"Come up here, taste and see that the Lord is good."*

It is the visionaries *"God's delegated representative or representatives"* that have been set and appointed by God over the spiritual house, who are responsible for seeing that identity is fashioned in the hearts and minds of all spiritual sons that have both joined and become jointed to the God vision. All five-fold ministers are called to fatherhood, though not all are called to father "oversee" a spiritual house. Those who are called to father *"oversee"* a spiritual house are ultimately responsible and held accountable for the raising and releasing of God's sons into their destiny in Christ. They are also responsible for the ministry that comes forth out of all five-fold gifts *"Governing elders"*, general elders and deacons within the spiritual family as well as all spiritual sons. Though all five-fold ministers are called to impart the gift of God into the lives of the spiritual sons, only God's delegated representative or representatives appointed and set over the spiritual house by God, carry the responsibility of releasing the sons for works of service unto the Lord. Every believer, "son of God" must be joined and jointed to a spiritual father that has been set and appointed by God over a spiritual house, for a season of training, equipping and ultimately releasing into the hands of God to be used as He wills for effective works of service.

"If God's appointed man or woman over a spiritual family is the only five-fold gift given to the body, then how will the sons of God ever grow to full maturity?"

The spiritual father or fathers within a spiritual house must establish covenant relationship with the remaining gifts of God *"God's delegated representatives"* that are also needed to raise the spiritual sons to full maturity. There may be an apostle, prophet, evangelist, pastor or teacher, over a particular region or area that through covenant relationship continues to impart the gift that he or she has received by Christ, into the sons of another spiritual house or family. In this case the gift of God *"Five-Fold Minister"* outside of the spiritual house, through covenant relationship, would father the sons within that particular house.

How Spiritual Fathers Are Established Over a Spiritual House

Men and women can not arbitrarily decide to function as spiritual fathers or ascension gifts *"Five-fold minister,"* as head over a spiritual family. They must be called by God and then given a mandate and message, for the spiritual family that he or she has been appointed and then set over. Not every five-fold minister *"Christ's Delegated Representative"* is given a mandate to head out or oversee a spiritual family. Some apostles, prophets, evangelists, pastors and teachers, are called by Christ to help fulfill the vision and mandate that God has given to another, though every five-fold minister has a specific command or mandate given by Christ *"Fatherhood."* Fatherhood is reproducing Christ in the lives of God's sons through raising, equipping, and then releasing the sons to operate within the specific function or gifting of the spiritual father.

Once the issue of fatherhood has been dealt with *"In our hearts"* through the inspiration of the Holy Spirit, God's mandate will now become clear to His delegated representatives. The mandate will never change although the message that is entrusted to each individual father will differ in the lives of the sons. There are different facets of Christ, though each facet will always direct the sons toward Christ and the advancing of His Kingdom.

In the previous chapter, the statement was made; that it wasn't the Job or even the functional role of God's delegated representatives "Spiritual *Fathers*," to bring healing, deliverance, or even salvation to every family member of God's spiritual house "*Local and Universal Church.*" We used the example concerning Jesus telling the disciples to "*go down loose him and let him go.*" According to *Ephesians 4:12*, we can clearly see that the functional role and even the mandate by God-given to the spiritual fathers, is to "Equip or prepare God's sons to do works of service." Like Moses "Before elders were appointed over Israel", within church as we've known it, many men and women of God are carrying more of a load then they were ever intended to carry. It's time we gain a true understanding of the functional role that we as ministers of the gospel of the kingdom of God are called to function-operate within. We then need to raise the sons of God up in order to handle different responsibilities, within their God-given calling and gifting in Christ. As men and women of God, we must enter into a place of rest, found only in the Lord.

As we enter into God's rest, we'll no longer strive or labor with the works of God though we'll align ourselves with His plan, purpose, and design for our lives, according to biblical patterns. Then that which we've been striving against will become a place of peace and restfulness. Many men and women within Church as we've known it, continually try to operate not only in their God-given function, but the function of many others as well. Though their hearts are pure, they are still out of order; therefore the task that lay ahead of them has become impossible to complete.

As we've seen within the life of Moses, his heart was right concerning his desire to minister to the children of Israel from sun up to sun down. Even though Moses' motives were pure, he was still out of order. Moses alone was incapable of effectively ministering to all of God's people. If not stopped, the exercise of singularity of ministry would have lead to the destruction of both Moses and all of Israel. No matter where we're called to operate or function in ministry—whether as support to a visionary or as God's delegated representatives, there is no place in God's divine order and godly government, for singularity of ministry. *"Exodus 18:13-27* <u>Jethro</u> *Principle"* [64]

"It's possible to turn your wilderness into an oasis, though only through operating within the functional role that you were first called by Christ Jesus to function within."

Releasing Spiritual Sons for a Season

We must begin to see and understand the need for the functional role of spiritual fathers, within the spiritual family *"Local Church, Spiritual House."* As a five-fold minister you have been given a mandate and command by God Himself, to raise, equip and release the sons of God to do the work of ministry. Sons will come in many shapes and sizes. Spiritual sons will be presented to the spiritual father with many different character flaws. As new fathers, we must not become overwhelmed with the responsibility of, equipping, raising and releasing, the sons who have greater flaws then others.

Remember that God will join the heart of a spiritual father to a spiritual son, through the unction and leading of the Holy Spirit. Once a father-son relationship has been established, the father now holds the responsibility for exposing the son to the remaining gifts of God, in order for the son to grow to full maturity.

There may be times when spiritual sons could actually be released for a season of preparation within a spiritual house *"Local Church"* of another Gift of God "Five-fold Minister," a minister that walks in accountability through covenant relationship with the spiritual father within the spiritual house of the sons. When releasing sons for further impartation, it should be to allow another functional office, *"five-fold minister"* to impart God's gift into their lives. Remember that a man or woman functioning within the office of an apostle, prophet, evangelist, pastor or teacher isn't capable of bringing sons into full maturity. Spiritual sons need the impartation of the remaining functional offices. Once a son has been released for a season of equipping through another gift of God, then that five-fold gift has now taken on the responsibility of fatherhood.

God's Spiritual Business

"Spiritual fathers will only become as successful as their spiritual sons."

Many men and women of God feel intimidated or threatened when someone with a heart for God begins to gain understanding and learns to walk in God's ways. You see it's our *"position"* that we are trying to protect, through our lack of enthusiasm for those that have a heart for the things of God. As fathers, our only joy should be to see the sons grow up to become greater then we could ever be.

"As long as we're bound by insecurities and fears related to the approval of man, then we'll never qualify to raise God's sons."

"A manager is only as successful as his employees." It's

the responsibility of the manager within a natural business, to train, equip, and then release his or her employees to do the work they were trained and hired to perform. This is an excellent parallel to the functional role of a spiritual father within the spiritual family "*House*." So let's look at this picture another way.

The five-fold gifts given to the Church "*You and I*," are the managers over God's spiritual business "Spiritual Family." The sons of God are the employees within this spiritual business and with the right training could possibly become managers one day as well. So as we begin to look at God's business within the structure of church as we've know it, it's clear to see that many managers are not functioning within their proper designated responsibilities. The saddest part concerning the lack of managers "five-fold" properly functioning within their God-given responsibilities is that all the blame has been placed upon the shoulders of the saints. It's no wonder why saints continue to walk within the same mentality throughout every generation. The truth is the saint in today's world is nothing more then a reproduction of what the five-fold gifts have willfully produced.

"Church as we've known it is powerless to change, unless leadership as we've known it changes."

Since before 100AD the Church "*You and I* has slowly fallen out of the order of God. God is presently restoring His Church back to Divine Order and Godly Government. God is establishing through the functional office of the Apostle and Prophet a solid foundation upon which the true Church of Jesus Christ is being built.[65] It's important for men and women of God to see and understand the restoration process of the five-fold ministry back to the Church of Jesus Christ. God has previously restored the functional office of the pastor, teacher, evangelist and prophet back to His Church.

God is presently restoring the last functional office of the five-fold gifts, the functional office of the apostle. All gifts operate in different functions and therefore all gifts are vital for the progression of the Church of Jesus Christ. Though God has given the responsibility within the body of Christ to the apostles and prophets to lay a solid foundation on the revelation of Christ Jesus, in which the rest of God's house *"universal Church"* is built.[66] Neither the apostle nor prophet has more responsibilities then the other five-fold gifts, within the body of Christ.

There is a reason that the apostles and prophets have been chosen by God to lay a solid foundation along with Christ Jesus the chief cornerstone. The functional role of the Prophet is to declare God's plan, purpose, and intent over kings, nations and governments. The functional role of the Apostle is to administrate or bring a decree to the spoken or declared word of the prophet. Apostles and prophets work hand and hand, establishing through Christ Jesus a foundation for godly living. Remember within the chapter "Hannah's Cry" we discussed the function of both the apostle and prophet? And how we as fathers must continue to live and be led by the spirit of God in order to administrate the spoken word of God, into the lives of the sons.

Before you're a spiritual father, you are first a son of God, empowered by the Holy Spirit. You are capable of being used in any way as the Holy Spirit wills. So if you are truly called to the five-fold ministry, then you're first and foremost responsibility is to raise and release the sons of God into their God-given destiny. Therefore God will not leave you as orphans, though through His Son "Christ", He has empowered you to fulfill His plan for your life, and the lives of His sons.

Can Women Become Spiritual Fathers

For most people it's hard to imagine a woman ministering behind the pulpit, though if she's ministering outside on the streets, then it's ok. The fact is that there are many insecure men of God within the structure of church, as we've known it. These men have lacked the true identity that is both imparted and developed through spiritual fathers.

"Are we not all sowing into the same field?"

"Are we not all working toward the same outcome?"

"Have we not all come unto salvation the same way through the blood of Jesus?"

"Is God no respecter of persons?"

These are just a few questions that we as the male gender need to ask, before we continue to elevate ourselves as ministerial giants. See the truth is; that if not for the love, patience and long suffering of women within the body of Christ, many of you that are reading this book wouldn't be where you are today.

> But if Christ is in you, your body is dead because of sin, yet your spirit is alive because of righteousness. And if the spirit of Him who raised Jesus from the dead is living in you, He who raised Christ from the dead will also give life to your mortal bodies through His spirit, who lives in you. (Romans 8:10-11 *NIV*)

> I can do all things through Christ that strengthens me. (Philippians 4:13 *KJV*)

As a New Testament Church we are no longer called to live or look at God's people within the confines of the natural flesh though this seems to be one of the hardest areas for both men and women of God to overcome. It has to do with the fact of not willing to let go of the old thinking in order to walk in the true revelation of Christ Jesus. There is no possible way to adequately cover this topic at this time, though there will be another time, to clearly lay a strong scriptural pattern for "Women in ministry." We must continue to challenge our old patterns of thinking.

Deborah the Prophetess "The Prophet of God"
Remember Deborah "The Prophetess" in the Old Testament. Deborah was called by God to be a judge to Israel, given a mandate to declare God's word to Barak concerning the army of Israel.

> And Deborah a Prophetess the wife of Lapidoth, she judged Israel at that time. (Judges 4:4 *KJV*)

Not only was Deborah called to the functional office of a Prophet, she was also the wife of Lapidoth. As you can see, there is a lot of material that would need to be laid out in order to uncover the spiritual truths of women in ministry. At this time I've chosen to expand on the spiritual truth of women in ministry from a New Testament point of view.

Taking a New Testament Look
God has called His New Testament sons to live according to the spirit, so that we won't fulfill the lust of the flesh. In other words, we can't afford to live according to the flesh, or the mindsets of natural man. *Romans 8:10* clearly states that those who have received life through God's spirit are no longer bound to the flesh, sin, and death. God's spirit makes us alive, which enables us to live according to *Romans 12*, as living sacrifices unto Father God.

If we'd only remove the blinders that we've place over our own eyes, we would see that through the eyes of God all things are possible. *John 4:24* says "*God is spirit and those who worship Him must worship Him in spirit and truth.*" So you see that God is not moved by the gender of His messenger, though the heart of men and women moves God. We must understand that as a spirit being, there is nothing we can't accomplish through the power of the Holy Spirit. It's vital for the restoration of God's Church, that we stop limiting God to our own ways of thinking.

> For my thoughts are not your thoughts, neither are your ways my ways declares the Lord, as the heavens are higher then the earth, so are my ways higher then your ways; and my thoughts higher then your thoughts.(Isaiah 55:8-9 *NIV*)

> As the rain and the snow comes down from heaven, and do not return to it without watering the earth and making it bud and flourish, so that it yields seed for the sower and bread for the eater. So is my word that goes out from my mouth: it will not return to me empty, but will accomplish what I desire and achieve the purpose of which I sent it. (Isaiah 55:10-12 *NIV*)

It's important to see the parallel in the spirit, to the natural truth that was conveyed within verses 10-12 in Isaiah. God is saying that once His word is spoken, it's now released to accomplish God's plan, purpose, and intent within the lives of others; therefore it won't return empty "void." We must see that within this scripture there is no distinction in gender, concerning who is authorized to speak His word. Though as the male gender, we've somehow come to the conclusion that this word is only for us.

I know that within this passage of scripture it's referring to God speaking, but allow me to ask you a question. *Have you ever heard the audible voice of God?* Most of you at this point are saying "N*o, though I would love to*." Well, allow me to shine some light on the other side of the coin. We have all heard the audible voice of God. Why, because God has chosen to use men and women with a true heart, desiring His will and ways, to speak through.

"Are we not the voice of God to the nations?"

Just allow this to sink in for a moment. What makes the male gender so great? Nothing; They have receive salvation from their sinful nature, the same way as the female gender. Yet the church, as we've known it continues to condemn women for operating in God-given authority through the power of the Holy Spirit.

> You are all sons of God through faith in Christ Jesus, for all of you who were baptized in Christ have clothed yourselves with Christ. There is neither Jew nor Greek, slave nor free, **male nor female, for you are all one in Christ Jesus**.
> (Galatians 3:26-28 *NIV*)

As we've seen throughout this segment, there is clearly evidence according to the word of God, concerning women within functional office in ministry. We must understand that the old laws *"mindset of man"* has passed away, and the life we live, we now live in the spirit of the one who established the New Covenant, *"Christ Jesus."* *"No longer I live but Christ now lives in me,"* As the church of Jesus Christ, we can't allow His death to have been in vain. We must understand that Christ carries both female and male characteristics and function, though that means that the male gender carries through Christ, female responsibilities and characteristics, *"Spiritual Mother."*

As for the question **"Can women become spiritual fathers?" Absolutely!** We have no problem believing that women are called by God to become teachers, which is a functional office that seems unthreatening to the male gender. Then we must understand that the functional office of a teacher is one of the five-fold gifts that Christ gave to His body. Therefore we must understand that women can become spiritual fathers, so this book applies to women as well.

Why Sons of God

The word of God relates to the term "sons of God" for a very simple reason. As we've discussed in earlier chapters the male gender's functional role in reproduction is to carry the natural seed and release the seed in order to reproduce natural offspring. As the body of Christ, our functional role is to carry the seed of God and then sow His seed into the lives of others in order to reproduce the nature of God. Its simple truths like this, which we seem to make harder than they really are to understand

Next Step after restoring The Five-Fold Functional Offices

"Unless the hearts of the five-fold ministers of God's word are changed throughout our world concerning the raising and releasing of God's sons, then the message within this book is useless. Therefore God will have to wait for another generation to turn the hearts of the fathers to the children and the hearts of the children to the fathers."

God is raising up apostles and prophets that will carry the father-son message to the nations, and will declare and administrate God's word with love to the five-fold ministers, through training and equipping the gifts of God concerning Divine Order and True Godly Government. Only once the five-fold ministers have received and begin walking within the true godly structure concerning spiritual family, will the rest of the body of Christ begin to properly be equipped to do the work of ministry.

"A shepherd must lead his or her sheep, though if the shepherd has no Idea where he or she is going, then neither the shepherd nor the sheep will ever arrive."

Reproducing Godly Offspring

Then God said, "let the land produce vegetation: seed-bearing plants and trees on the land that bear fruit with seed in it, according to their various kind." And it was so the land produced vegetation: plants bearing seed according to their own kinds and trees bearing fruit with seed in it according to their kind. And God saw that it was good. (Genesis 1:11-12 *NIV*)

According to the principle found within Genesis, everything must reproduce after its own kind. Therefore if you plant an apple seed, you will reap a harvest of apple trees that in due season will bear forth apples. This is the same principle for raising spiritual sons of God. Remember that each and every son has a God-given destiny, and it's the responsibility of the spiritual fathers to help draw out his or her destiny. We need to understand that the gifts of God "five-fold ministers" are responsible for sowing the seed of God into the sons in order for the seed to reproduce itself within the hearts of the sons.

Once the seed *"God's Word"* has had a chance to grow and mature, the manifestation of the sown seed could be an apostle, prophet, evangelist, pastor or teacher. As fathers we must continually keep in mind that the very one we've been entrusted to raise could be a Prophet called to declare God's word over kings, nations and governments, or an apostle that will be called to administrate peace treaties to the governments of our world. We must never stop looking with the eyes of God at the sons that have been entrusted in our care. To the natural eye they may only appear to look as Gideon though within the eyes of God, they are truly mighty men and women of valor.

Just like an apple seed, five-fold ministers are called to reproduce after their own kind. Therefore fathers will not only produce the Christ nature within the hearts of sons, but also at times their same functional office. It's important to understand that men and women, *"whether walking within Divine Order and Godly Government or not,"* have no right to position sons into functional office. Men and women within church as we've know it, seek to pass out positions in order to keep the sons of God, bound and chained in the name of religion. Only Christ has the ability to set and appoint His sons into functional office.[67]

We, as fathers, may see a certain function in which the sons have progressed in, although there are still no grounds for the fathers to title them with a certain functional office. We, as fathers, are called to direct and instruct the sons of God into their God-given destiny, which means that the sons must be raised to maturity, in order to hear clearly concerning his or her God-given functional role of operation within the family. As the sons gain an understanding as to their functional role within the spiritual family, then they'll begin to automatically walk in their God-given function.

There must be the reproducing of functional office within the spiritual family of God. God's plan is for the Gifts of God "five-fold ministers" to multiply the Christ likeness, as well as functional office within the sons. The majority of the sons will be raised up to fulfill different functional roles and offices, within the body of Christ rather than the functional role and office of their primary father "Delegated representative or representatives over a spiritual house". We need to understand that God's plan is for apostles to reproduce apostles, and for prophets to reproduce prophets. Though this can only take place, as God entrusts a spiritual son to a spiritual father that has already been called and appointed by God to walk one day in a particular functional office.

CHAPTER SIX

God's Divine Structural Order and Godly Government

Today, there is a turning within the hearts of God's people taking place. Though we must align our will with God's word in order to complete the turning of the hearts of men and women back to God's divine structural order and government. As the body of Christ we need to start ordering our conversation in such a way that we begin to speak solutions before we ever face the problem.[68] As we begin to speak to those things, which aren't as though they were, we'll start to align our will *"spirit of man"* with God's will *" the Holy Spirit."* Coming into this next chapter, we, as the Church of the living God, must remove all preconceived ideas concerning who we've thought God is, and how we've thought ministry should be run. I know that the Holy Spirit will open the hearts of all those that read this chapter, in order to bring the revelation of Christ Jesus concerning God's Divine Order and Godly Government.

As believers, we're called to live according to the word

of God. Through allowing the word "Christ" to always become our first and final authority, regardless of the situations we face every day within our lives though most believers tend to live as a product of their environment. Our world aside from God seems to understand no other way in which to deal with daily trials outside of reacting upon their emotions and feelings.[69] As sons of God, we're called to be *"slow to speak," "quick to hear,"* and *"slow to answer."* This allows the body of Christ the ability to respond with godly wisdom, instead of reacting with worldly sorrow.[70] *Romans 8:14* tells us that as long as we're spirit-led and spirit-directed, then we've earned the right to be called the true sons of God.

God has commanded His five-fold gifts to raise, equip, and then release His sons to do the work of ministry though before we can truly begin to see the five-fold gifts fulfilling God's command, first each of the five-fold gifts must be restored back to God's Divine Order and Godly Government.[71] The present day five-fold gifts must stop building church, as we've known it. Church, as we've known it, continues to reproduce after its own kind. As a direct result it's created many insecure men and women within ministry today. Leaders, only capable of sowing the seeds of man, where we're now starting to reap the harvest of their sown seeds, "the sons of man." Only after the five-fold gifts start to align themselves up with God's true plan and purpose for His Church, "can their hearts turn towards receiving spiritual sons."

We must come to the place where we can say; "**Enough is enough!**" I know that everyone who is reading this book understands what the Holy Spirit is saying. The question is will you, like John the Baptist, stand up and call sin *"Disobedience"* and righteousness *"Obedience?"* Church as we've known it has willfully lived with the color gray for so long, that we have actually forgotten what any other color looks like. Jesus said "*A lukewarm Christian I will spew out of my mouth, therefore I would rather you be hot or cold*." The days of building our own kingdoms are over! Apostles, prophets, evangelists, pastors and teachers must stop building the kingdoms of man and start to build the kingdom of God. Listen to the spirit of the Lord. We must stop playing church and gain the understanding that you and I are the Church of Jesus Christ!

"*The problem with church as we've know it, is the fact that we're all to preoccupied building our own kingdoms, that we can't seem to find the time to build the kingdom of God*."

As long as we continue to place our main focus upon building church, we'll never be able to advance the kingdom of God. Building church focuses upon the multiplicity of numbers, and not on singularity concerning individual people. If our desire is to advance the kingdom of God, then we can't afford to look at people as just another number. We must begin looking at them with the eyes and potential of God. Remember that each individual whether saved or lost, has a God-given destiny. It's time the five-fold gifts start speaking into the destiny of God's sons, so that they'll be effectively equipped to walk with God's power and demonstration within the earth.

"Without reproducing spiritual sons then there is no tomorrow, therefore the future generations must rely on the spiritual fathers that are ready to raise God's sons in this generation."

Church as we've known it must be reformed back to God's Divine Order and Godly Government. As the body of Christ it's important that we allow this chapter to penetrate our hearts, in order to move us towards change. This chapter is vital concerning the restoration of church as we've known it.

Decline in Church History

It's important that we understand the decline in Church history. Therefore we'll not only learn from where we have come, though we will also learn where the Church of Jesus Christ is heading.

1. False ministries went unhindered 2 *Peter 2:1-9, Acts 20:28-30*
   A. There was the lack of accountability.

2. Self- willed believers 2 *Peter 2:10*
   A. There was a lack of submission.

3. Lost the hunger for truth *1 Timothy 4:1-2*
   A. Lost the fire of God.

4. Spiritual compromises *2 Timothy 4:3-4*
   A. One foot in one foot out.

5. De-emphases on character *2 Peter 1:3-11*
   A. No values.

6. Carnal indulgences Ephesians *2:3, 2 Peter 3:3*
   A. Lust of the eyes.

As you can see, these are just a few of the areas that actually led to the fall of the body of Christ. I would like to layout a time line concerning the events that took place, which eventually dragged the body of Christ slowly into the dark ages.

30-100 AD-   The body of Christ had witnessed the apostolic ministry in power and demonstration, also within this particular time spanned was the witness of the death of the last disciple called by Jesus Christ "John"

100 AD-   After 100 AD there has been no evidence of the apostolic ministry continuing.

130 AD-   Now the once powerful and life changing impartation concerning the laying on of the hands had now become a ritual as the time began to pass the body of Christ became less and less productive.

140 AD-   We saw the last ministry of the Prophet, for no longer was there a man or woman that would be willing to allow God to speak through them as a mouthpiece. The very ability to even utter a prophetic word had now become rare.

150 AD-   During this time there was a lack of operating within the gifts of the Holy Spirit, as we know the Holy Spirit is vital to the lives of a believer.

160 AD-   The plurality of leadership began to fade away, though we were never called to operate in singularity of ministry. (God is presently restoring His Church back to team ministry.)

180 AD-   As Roman government took over; the

local church gathering was now disappearing.

187 AD- The first infant baptism took place, in which the infant was sprinkled instead of submerged under water.

200 AD- Though the church had a form of godliness, it was denied the power, as water baptism in the name of the Lord Jesus Christ was now being denied. (This was mostly the direct result of Pope Steven.)

210 AD- The doctrine of the Priesthood was being denied, as the priestly clergy began to elevate themselves higher in their faith.

225 AD- Church membership had now become a matter of agreeing with a creed and was no longer based upon conversion.

240 AD- Holiness had disappeared and now worldliness had infiltrated the church (Body of Christ)

350 AD- Constantine became ruler of the Roman Empire and Christianity was made the state religion. Separation by faith was no longer essential as many heathens were forced to consent to Christianity by the sword.

380 AD- Rome was made to be the final authority by Theodosius in church matters thus

the church enter into a period known as the "**DARK AGES.**"

After the dark ages, Church continued to plunge deeper and deeper into a form of Godliness but still denying the power, as God's kingdom was denied and men became kings.

It's important for the church to understand where it's been in order to appreciate what God is restoring and reforming. Though the Church of Jesus Christ fell into the dark ages, God still had a plan for His sons. We're truly living in the greatest days. God is presently working by His spirit within the hearts of His sons; as Christ is presently ruling and reigning as king of His Kingdom "*You and I.*"

Divine Order

It's not hard to see why the church is in a time of reformation. We have strayed so far from the ancient paths "*True Authentic Christianity*" that only God could bring us back. This is why you've heard over and over again throughout this book, that church as we've known it must change. Remember when David brought the Ark of the Covenant back to Israel, and how he was so excited.[72] He had even prepared a new cart, one that was better then the cart the Philistines had made. Everything seemed to go just as planed, when all of a sudden Uzzah reached up to steady the Ark of the Covenant, and was struck dead.

David was full of faith. He also had a strong desire to bring back the Ark of the Covenant to God's people. Then why was Uzzah killed for touching it? It doesn't appear to make sense why Uzzah would've been struck dead, if his heart and motives were as pure as David's was?

David was ignorant as to the order of how God had instructed the Ark of the Covenant "*God's presence*" to be carried. Therefore even though David's heart was pure, he was still out of order. David lacked the understanding concerning the proper order for ushering in the presence of God. It's important for us to see that the ark had to be steadied, because the ox that was pulling the presence of God "*Stumbled.*" The ox and cart are symbolic of the "*order of man.*" According to what we've already learned, the order of man only builds the kingdoms of man. Therefore every kingdom of man that doesn't represent the kingdom of God will be shaken, or *stumble.*

> Tell Zerubbabel Governor of Judah that I will shake the heavens and the earth. I will overturn royal thrones and shatter the power of the foreign kings. I will overthrow chariots and their drivers; horses and their riders will fall, each by the sword of his brother. (Haggai 2:21-22 *NIV*)

> At that time His voice shook the earth, but now He has promised, "Once more I will shake not only the earth but also the heavens." The words "Once more" indicate the removing of what can be shaken—that is, created things—so that what cannot be shaken may remain. Therefore since we are receiving a Kingdom that cannot be shaken, let us be thankful and so worship God acceptably with reverence and awe, for our God is a consuming fire.(Hebrews 12:26-28 *NIV*)

"Walking within the order of man and trying to control or steady the presence of God, will lead to death."

Church as we've known it was conceived and birthed

out of the dark ages, into a generation that has never truly understood God's structural order. Men and women must learn to see the Word of God with the eyes of God. Having the vision of God is vital, in order to rediscover God's Divine Order for ushering in His presence.

The orders of man *"Tradition and Religion"* cause the church to walk in the flesh and lose sight of the reverent fear of God. Thus church, as we've known it; begins to take the things of God lightly. This mentality brings about death within the body of Christ. We should stop and ask ourselves why we're running church the way we are? Most men and women would be shocked to hear God's response. Is it possible that we're simply following in the footsteps of our predecessors? Who would have only been following in the footsteps of their predecessors. Could our spiritual pattern be nothing more then a learned behavior passed down from generation to generation? Are we just like King David; his heart was right though he *"because of the practice of man that was established before him"* was unable to bring the presence of God *"Ark"* back to Israel.

God's Order for Carrying the Ark of the Covenant

You see King David had not been raised knowing how to usher *"God's Presence-God's Ark"* in the true order of God. God's order for carrying the Ark of the Covenant was upon the shoulders of the priest. We, as the church of today, have not been raised to know the true order of God, the establishing of God's Glory "His Manifested Presence" within His earth.

> David was afraid of the Lord that day, and
> said how can the ark of the Lord ever come
> to me? (2 Samuel 6:9 *NIV*)

Once David understood that he was *"out of order,"* he

then turned to the only one that could teach him the true order for bringing the presence of God back to Israel, "Father God." The Ark of the Covenant had been lost for many generations. Therefore David was incapable of speaking to anyone in his generation concerning the true order for bringing God's presence back to His people. Before learning from God the true order, David had a strong desire within his heart to please God. So while attempting to bring the Ark of the Covenant back to Israel, David appeared to have done all the right preparations. There were singers and dancers "worshipers" in front of the Ark, leading the way, while both men and women lifted up their voices before the Lord. Though everything seemed right, they were still out of order. Why? They were still not following the true pattern or blueprint for bringing God's presence back to His people.

We can see today, that many sons of God have a true desire within their hearts to usher in God's presence though they've not been raised within a generation that understands the true structural order of God. There is only one way that we'll be able to gain true understanding concerning God's Divine Order. We, as the Church of Jesus Christ, need to fall on our faces before God. We need to begin crying out for the true structure and order that's needed to usher in the presence of God back to His Church. [73]

> May God Himself the God of peace, sanctify you through and through. May your whole spirit soul and body be kept blameless at the coming of our Lord Jesus Christ. (1 Thessalonians 5:23 *NIV*)

As we've learned within previous chapters. The order of God within the lives of all man; is "*Spirit*" "*Soul*" and "*Body*." Church, as we've known it has tried everything it knows, to usher in the presence of God, through operating within the flesh "*Body*." Therefore as long as we continue to strive toward perfection in the natural, we deny the Holy Spirit the opportunity to bring the manifestation of perfection within our spiritual walk. It's impossible to teach and preach God's word and expect to see God results, while at the same time denying the power of the Holy Spirit. It's vital to the Church of Jesus Christ that we begin to acknowledge the necessity of the Holy Spirit within the lives of all believers. No longer are we confined to the limitations of the natural, for we've now been clothed with immortality within the spirit. [74]Also we've been given the ability through the Holy Spirit, to receive the mind of Christ. [75]

> However it is written; "No eye has seen, No ear has heard, No mind has conceived, what God has prepared for those that love Him. But God has revealed it to us by His spirit. The spirit searches all things even the deep things of God. (1 Corinthians 3:9-19 *NIV*)

This scripture was never intended to describe a place or a natural dwelling. Though as the true Church of Jesus Christ, we need to see that this passage is relaying that it's a privilege as spirit beings, to be found in Christ Jesus. The eye of the flesh can't see. The ear of the flesh can't hear. The mind of the flesh can't understand the things that Christ is speaking and showing His true Church "*You and I*." We must ask ourselves this question. "*Are we as the body of Christ practicing the theology and doctrines of men instead of true Christology?*" **Christology**, *are the Biblical truths and patterns of Christ our supreme ruler, who has authority over all things*. It's time we reevaluate church, as we've known it. We must let go of our old thought patterns that we've established and allow Christ the ability to build His Church.

Trust in the Lord with all your heart. Lean not on your own understanding, in all your ways acknowledge Him and He shall direct your path. (1 Corinthians 3:9-10 *NIV*)

Godly Government

"The Government of God is essentially family, family structure and family based. When we as the church of Jesus Christ stop being family, then we no longer walk within God's Government. Therefore we as the Church have now become nothing more then a glorified religious organization."

Church as we've known it appears to be more like a glorified membership club. With our rights reserved through paying our weekly dues, to change anything we don't agree upon within our organization. Man has never been given a mandate to build his or her church. "What about Paul the Apostle, was he not called to establish churches?" **APSO-LUTLY NOT!** Paul was commissioned or given a mandate by Christ to quit kicking against the brick.[76] Christ was saying, "Stop building your own kingdom of man and start to build the kingdom of God," "family."

As long as we continue to build upon the foundations of sinking sand, then we're no different from Saul, when he was persecuting the Christians. We need to see that the ministry of Christ, through Paul the Apostle, was directed 100% toward the changing of the lives of individuals. Paul was a bondservant of Christ, though only for the development of the lives of individuals. Therefore his work was not to erect a church building made out of dead and lifeless material though his work was to erect a spiritual house, made with living stones. He did establish places of meeting. Although never focusing on the material building. Though focusing upon the raising and equipping of the sons of God, to do the work of ministry. [77]

The functional Role of an Apostle has never been to

build Churches or even congregations. The functional role has been to establish within the hearts of men and women divine order *"True biblical patterns for daily living"* and godly government *"Family- biblical covenant relationships."* We must understand the pattern in which Paul the Apostle used in order to change the lives of thousands. He understood that he had to reach one family at a time. Then he could reach one local gathering at a time, as well now carrying the ability to reach one city at a time and one nation or country at a time. "It's a grievance to our Lord Jesus Christ, for the wisdom of man to label the work of the Chief Apostle "Christ," as a church builder *"Planter."* Lord Jesus, open our eyes to your spiritual plan within our lives as your Church."

> Let us not give up meeting together, as some
> are in the habit of doing, but let us encourage
> one another, and all the more as you see the
> day approaching.(Hebrews 10:25 NIV)

It's vital that the body of Christ meet together in order to build one another up in the most Holy of faith.[78] Within church as we've known it our main focus seems to be directed away from individual people. We've placed the facility and the income needed in order to continue running our own agendas and programs for self-elevation, above the sons of God, above God's governmental structure, *"Family."*

Church, as we've known it is presently operating based upon the governmental structure of man, **"Democracy."** Democracy is *a government, in which supreme power is exercised, directly by the people or their elected agents.* The Church of Jesus Christ must be restored to operate under the governmental structure of **"Theocracy,"** a *form of government in which a deity is recognized as the supreme ruler.* There is no wonder the gates of hell are prevailing against church, as we've known it. We seem to continually walk in the order of man, while operating within the governments of this world. For this very reason, we as the body of Christ must be reformed back to true biblical pattern which must be laid by the functional work of both the Apostle and Prophet working hand and hand, with Christ Jesus as the Chief corner stone.

In *Matthew 16:1-16* Jesus asks the question. "*Who do people say the son of man is?*" The disciples answered, "*Some say Elijah or John the Baptist, others say Jeremiah.*" Jesus replied, "*What about you, who do you say I am?*"

> Simon Peter answered "You are the Christ the Son of the living God." Jesus replied "Blessed are you Simon son of Jonah, for this was not revealed to you by man, but by my Father in Heaven." And I tell you that you are Peter, and upon this rock I will build my Church, and the gates of hades will not overcome it. I will give you the keys of the kingdom of heaven; whatever you bind on earth will be bound in heaven, and whatever you loose on earth, will be loosed in heaven. (Matthew 16:16-19 *NIV*)

Divorce is one way, in which the gates of hell are prevailing against the Church today? The rate of divorce within church is unbelievable. We're seeing families that were raised in the structure of church, unable to overcome simple relational problems, thus giving birth to dysfunctional families.

"How is it possible for a wife that teaches Sunday school and her husband that's served as a deacon for 12 years, to file for a divorce?"

"As long as we're walking within the governmental structure of man *"democracy,"* we're denying all that is true concerning God's governmental structure *"Theocracy."* Therefore we must gain the understanding that the structure in which church is operating in today is "fallible." It's time to allow Christ once again to reign supreme as the head of His body *"You and I."* For many generations we've seen the effects of the body leading the head. Therefore the body has now become dysfunctional. We have to see that church, as we've known it, is the breeding ground for the religious traditions of man. We know that the traditions of man make the word of God to no effect. The traditions of man make Christ "the Son of the living God" to no effect **"POWER-LESS ON THE EARTH."** [79]

You may ask why haven't we seen this pattern before now? The reason is because many men and women were never taught to read God's word. As well, as coming to a conclusion through the Holy Spirit, as to what Christ was saying. Since we were old enough to gain some kind of understanding concerning church, as we've known it, we've been told that the preacher is *"ALWAYS RIGHT."* Therefore if the man or woman of God says it, then it must be true. This mindset carries the power to pull the Church of Jesus Christ back into the *"DARK AGES."* It's time for the body of Christ to rise up and say **"NO MORE!"** Are you not as tired as I am of seeing a form of Godliness though always being denied the God-given power for change? It's time for a renewal of the hearts of all men and women of God in order to live as the true sons of God.

"Who do we think we're kidding?" The world isn't fooled with our lack of character and manifestation of the love of God. If it weren't for both gullible and inse-cure believers, then church as we've known it, would become nonexistent."

Peter's response to the question that Jesus had asked *was "You are the Christ the Son of the living God."* Jesus responded *"Upon this rock I will build my church and the gates of hades will not overcome it."* You see Peter was not the rock. The rock was the revelation or understanding that Christ was the Son of the living God. Peter recognized the deity, the all-powerful, all knowing God, living within Jesus the son of man, *"who represented humanity."* The true Church of Jesus Christ must first and foremost be built solely upon the revelation or understanding of Christ "The Anointed One, The Son of God." As we begin to place Christ as the head of His family "CHURCH" once again, then we'll start to walk in God's Divine Order and Godly Government as His true Church.

> Any one, who loves his father or mother more then me, is not worthy of me, anyone who loves his son or daughter more then me is not worthy of me. And anyone who does not take his cross and follow me is not worthy of me. Whoever finds his life will lose it, and whoever loses his life for my sake will find it. (Matthew 10:37-39 *NIV*)

Keep in mind, that as the family of God, we're called to operate within the governmental structure of theocracy. Though only as we begin to decrease, will Christ the head start to increase and to His kingdom there will be no end.[80] We must understand that the kingdom of God is the reign, rule, and authority of Christ Jesus. It is the peace of God in the midst of all storms and the joy of God in the midst of all sorrows. The Kingdom of God is the power through Christ, to live a righteous lifestyle in the midst of unrighteous living. Christ Jesus is presently working within the hearts of all those that believe. Jesus said, "That my kingdom is not of this world" God's kingdom was never intended to be constructed or established upon natural or material things, if so then Jesus and His disciples would have fought for His kingdom.

"God's kingdom doesn't represent where we are, but rather who we are in Christ Jesus."

Who Will Restore God's Church?

> Your people will repair the ancient ruins and will raise up the age old foundations; you will be called the repair of broken walls, Restorer of streets of dwelling. (Isaiah 58:12 *NIV*)

We as the sons of God are called to rebuild the old waste places. Once again, I'd like to parallel the natural with the spiritual. Let's talk about the natural foundation that's required when building a house. Then relate it to the foundation of the New Testament Church. The foundation of the New Testament Church was *"strong," "solid," "unshakable"* and *"balanced,"* just as the foundation of a new house, were all familiar with the fact that after a number of years many natural foundations begin to settle. Settling causes them to crack and then become unbalanced. Though we need to understand that besides the settling, there are also other elements that have caused structural decay and destruction to natural foundations. Wind and rain both play a major role in the structural damage to natural foundations. Once all the elements have taken their toll, a natural foundation will lack the ability to stand.

This is a great picture to parallel with the Church, as we've known it. The first foundation of the church appeared to be strong, solid and unshakeable, "just like we had learned concerning the natural foundation," it collapsed. In time wind *"Order of man"* and rain *"religions*

Doctrines of man" along with other elements like; *gossip, jealousy* and *strife*, caused the foundation of the New Testament Church to become off balanced. We see that the end result was the same as within the natural foundation. The Church of Acts lacked the ability to stand. It's imperative that we understand the present day condition of church, as we've known it. Only then can we become motivated to repair the broken wall and rebuild the ancient ruins. We must allow God to work through each and every individual in order to restore the mentality of mans way of thinking, back to God's way of understanding though it cost all that you have, gain understanding.

So what are the ancient ruins we're called to rebuild? The ancient ruins are the pure truths of God's word that has been lost from the hearts of men and women since we were born. We must rebuild the hearts of men and women in ministry in order to receive God's true structure of operation, through the inspiration of the Holy Spirit. Concerning the walls, we as the body, are called to tare down the walls of hurt, pain and shame within the lives of God's sons. Remember it was never the responsibility of the five-fold gifts to heal, deliver and set God's sons free. As the body begins to love unconditionally through the power of the Holy Spirit, we'll begin to see the dividing walls of separation that men have erected, torn down.

> The spirit of the sovereign Lord is upon me, because the Lord has anointed me to preach good news to the poor. He has sent me to bind up the broken hearted, to proclaim freedom for the captives and release from darkness the prisoners." (Isaiah 61:1-2 *NIV*)

The spirit of the Lord holds the power to break all bondage within the lives of the sons of God though the greatest part of this truth is the fact that His spirit lives within all those who believe in the Lord Jesus Christ as Savior. We as believers have a lot to be thankful for, concerning the work of God's grace within our lives.

Remember in chapter three "Hannah's cry," concerning the milk which is the whole word of God. Also concerning the meat, that is the physical act of manifesting the kingdom of God. As the body of Christ, we have a responsibility to the rest of the world. Our responsibility involves a lot more then just sitting back and feeding ourselves upon the revelations of God's word. One of the purposes for God delivering us out of the kingdom of darkness was to manifest His love and power through us to the rest of the world.

> They will be called oaks of righteousness a planting of the Lord for the display of His splendor. They will rebuild the ancient ruins and restore the places long devastated, they will renew the ruin cities that have been devastated for generations. (Isaiah 61:3-4 *NIV*)

So what is this secret weapon that will annihilate the mislead direction of the enemy toward God's people? **THE SONS OF GOD!** God has chosen to torment the enemy, with the very ones the enemy has tormented. As the church is restored back to Divine Order and Godly Government, the sons of God "Oaks of righteousness" are responsible for manifesting the presence of God through the fruit of love, in order to heal the nations.

"CHURCH AS WE'VE KNOWN IT MUST CHANGE!"

CHAPTER SEVEN

The Difference between Fathers and Kings

In order for God to establish spiritual fathers within this generation, He must first dethrone all kings and their man made kingdoms within the body of Christ.[81] God is continually reforming His Church back to Divine Order and Godly Government. Kings and their kingdoms, has never been God's plan for His Church.

"What are the results of dethroning kings and their kingdoms?", the restoring and establishing of church, as we've known it back to Godly Government "Family Structure", starting with spiritual fathers. It's time we start to build the kingdom of God, with the sole purpose of becoming God's representatives throughout the earth. We as the body of Christ must completely sell out 100%, allowing Christ to reign as supreme authority over our lives "*as we submit to His will,*" no longer continuing to walk within the same structure of yesterday. One of the hardest things for most men and women of God to do is lean not on their own understanding but in all their way acknowledge Christ as supreme authority over their lives. With Christ reigning in

full authority over all aspects of our lives, then everything we do becomes an outward expression of our intimate relationship with Father God. We must begin to let go of our old ways of thinking, therefore allowing within our hearts, *"through the inspiration of the Holy Spirit,"* God's true structural patterns for raising and releasing the sons of God, to do the work of ministry.

> Praise be to the God and father of our Lord Jesus Christ, who has blessed us in the heavenly realms with every spiritual blessing in Christ. (Ephesians 1:3 *NIV*)

It's important to understand that in Christ all that is needed to raise the sons of God *"spiritual sons"* has already been given to spiritual fathers though fathers must continue to walk in obedience according to God's word. As spiritual fathers begin to walk in obedience to God's word through faith, they'll obtain the right to receive the spiritual truths that are needed to properly operate within their functional office.

Kings, through their lack of faith and obedience, have been denied the right to receive the spiritual truths of God's word that are needed in order to properly raise God's sons. Therefore the lifestyle of a king is not one that reflects or expresses outwardly the true nature or likeness of Christ.[82] Kings are raised to walk in a form of Godliness, though always denying the ability for God's power to manifest within their lives and the lives of those they are raising. Like the scribes and Pharisees, kings appear to be clean on the outside though the inside will tell a completely different story.[83] We'll always be able to recognize kings by the type of fruit they bear.[84] We can't recognize them by their gifts or anointing, only their fruit. A king is not capable of consistently walking within the fruit of the spirit, *"LOVE."*

Love is the fruit that qualifies the sons of God to operate

in true God-given authority. Love is the root of all things; therefore, all things must stem outwardly from love. Ministry must be a direct extension of God's love made manifest through His sons. As God's sons, we need to recognize the difference between spiritual fathers and kings.

This chapter is written as a warning to both men and women of God who have a true calling upon their lives though they have perverted the word of God for personal gain. As long as there is breath in your lungs, it's never too late to repent of selfish desires and humble yourselves before God.[85] "*All sheep have gone astray, each one unto his own way,*" The body of Christ, is paralleled throughout the word of God as sheep. As sheep seek guidance from their shepherd, so does, "*the sons of God*" seek guidance from the gift of God "The *Shepherd or Spiritual Father.*" A spiritual father is only a picture of our relationship with Father God; therefore the spiritual father is not our ultimate shepherd.[86]

We need to approach this chapter with the understanding that we no longer live according to the law of Judgement or the law of circumcision of the flesh. We now live according to the law of grace, "spirit life." Therefore our main goal within this chapter is to expose the deeds of flesh. While at the same time, bring restoration through the imparting of the Holy Spirit and "God's Grace." The reason we have kings and their own kingdoms within church, as we've known it, is the fact that the kings were raised without a shepherd, "*Spiritual father,*" walking in God's Divine Order and Godly Government. Most kings within church, as we've known it, were truly called into the ministry by Christ Jesus though without the love, of a spiritual father to help direct and instruct concerning their destiny in Christ.[87] Therefore, kings had no alternative but to try and raise themselves on their own.[88]

At one time or another, these men and women had godly motives, though no insight or direction concerning godly relationship.[89] There is a key to avoiding the painful and lonely road, in which a king walks down. This key is to establish right relationships with one another, through submitting to the authority of Christ within the life of another. We'll never walk in true God-given authority until we first learn to submit to God-given authority within the life of another.[90] As the body of Christ, we need to continually keep our eyes upon those things which are not seen, "eternal." [91] Therefore we'll not be caught up in "*the pride of life*" that says, "I will submit to no man." It's vital that we as the sons of God gain an understanding that the temporal material items such as cars, boats, houses, money, clothes and jewelry will all pass away, though the love of God is eternal.[92] As the true sons of God, we can't allow ourselves to focus upon the material needs of the flesh. We must not lose sight of the love of God, or we'll start to focus upon the love of money.[93] As stated all throughout this book, "Everything must reproduce after its own kind." Therefore whatever you sow, then you will reap or harvest.

"It's vital for the advancement of the Kingdom of God, that we expose the corrupt seed sown into the hearts of men and women by kings, and stop church, as we've known it, from reproducing counterfeit offspring."

Kingdoms of Man Are Not God's Plan

So all the elders of Israel gathered together and came to Samuel at Ramah. They said to him you are old and your sons do not walk in your ways; now appoint a king to lead us, such as all the other nations have. (1 Samuel 8:4-5 *NIV*)

Within chapter four "Eli's Sons of Unrestraint," we

learned that God had changed the order concerning priest-hood in the house of Eli. Samuel, who was the spiritual son of Eli, was now appointed by God to usher in the new estab-lished order of God. Therefore, as we have previously dis-cussed, Samuel was now the "mouthpiece of God" to the nations and thus a Prophet was born. God had now appointed Samuel to become Judge over all Israel.

Though Samuel walked in the ways of God, we've learned that his sons chose to turn from God's ways. With Samuel's sons turning from the ways of God, they'd now perverted the very functional office they were appointed to uphold. So as a direct result of Samuel's sons walking in disobedience to the ways of God, Israel was now requesting to be ruled by the governmental structure of the world in which they lived. Israel was requesting the rulership of a king instead of the God-given order of fatherhood. Israel chose within their hearts to become just like the rest of the world. They were willfully stepping outside of God's true structure of government. It's important to understand that Israel's reason for wanting a king was temporal or material. Israel was seeking the protection of a king, willing to fully place their trust and security within the fact that a king and his kingdom would not fail them.[94]

"Israel had placed their eyes upon those things which were temporal. They were blinded by the lack of their rever-ent fear of God, which led Israel to ignorantly seek the lead-ership and rule of a king."

Samuel tried to explain to Israel all that a natural king would require of them. He told them how a king would first number the people for a show of strength.

Isn't this exactly what church, as we've known it, has been doing, numbering the attendance and membership role and then judging the strength of "Their Ministry" accord-ing to the number of people that are presently attending?

Also Samuel explained to the elders of Israel that a king would send their sons off to war and cause them to run before his chariots and horses. Also the fact that a king would assign positions for the sons of Israel to walk or function in. A king would appoint some sons as commanders and some sons to plow their fields.

Once again it's not hard to see the parallel between the demands of a king and the functional operation of church, as we've known it. Just as a king, ministers all over the world have placed responsibilities upon their own shoulders. Responsibilities that require the elevation of men and women into ministerial positions based upon popularity, anointing and convenience. Though as we've learned, "Only Christ can set and appoint both men and women into functional office not a king."

Samuel also explained that a king would take his daughters and place them in functional roles. These roles would require them to cook and become perfumers for the pleasure of the king.

*Just like a king, men within church, as we've known it have failed to recognize the God-given potential of women in ministry. Therefore women are denied the ability to go off to war and fight the battle. Though as long as women want to stand on the sidelines and serve the warriors then that's ok. Well the truth is "**IT'S NOT OK**," women have as much right to function within their God-given anointing and gifts.*

Samuel continued; a tenth of your grain and of vintage will be given to his officials. Your maid and men servants and your choice cattle will also be required. After Israel had heard all from Samuel concerning what was to come, Israel still cried out for a king. They had denied the hand of God and were now crying out for the hand of man to become their deliverer. Though Samuel relayed all the repercussions that they'd suffer through the hands of a king, Israel would still not listen to reason, because of their backsliding condition: Israel had already removed their eyes from God.

Church, as we've known it, is still operating within this very same pattern. We've denied the voice of God's instruction and continue to cry out for the rule of a king. Although kings within church as we've known it promise to protect all who dwell within their kingdom, that is an impossible promise to keep.

"Every kingdom of this world will be shaken and only the kingdom of God will stand."

Many kings are erecting their own fortified kingdoms. Though their kingdoms have the illusion of being built upon a solid foundation, in reality they're built upon sinking sand.[95] There can only be one king within a kingdom. As sons of God we belong to the kingdom of God, where Christ is presently ruling and reigning as king of his kingdom *"You and I."* Christ alone will build His Church. It's time for all believers to seek God for His true biblical patterns, so that we as the sons of God can begin to walk within our full potential.

Characteristics of a King

Kings are elevated by the wind of the people in which they're ruling over.

The function of a king is to reign, rule, and walk in complete authority within his kingdom. Just as a king will reign and rule over his kingdom, many men and women of God within the nations are reigning and ruling over God's people. While at the same time keeping them; bound within their kingdoms of man. As men and women of God, we must always understand that Christ is the head of every natural and spiritual house. Therefore as God's delegated representatives to the people, we must first and foremost submit our fleshly desires to God. You see, just like many that are reading this book, kings are masters of control and manipulation. They speak with eloquent speech and always dress for success, more concerned about their appearance then their character. This type of leadership is a stench in the nostrils of God.

As God's delegated representatives, we must conduct ourselves as ambassadors of Christ Jesus to the rest of the world. Therefore, we must present ourselves through our attire, posture, and speech as if we were meeting the Queen of England or the President of the United States, though we must not focus entirely upon our attire, posture, and speech. We need to constantly check our heart attitudes and motives behind why and how we are presenting ourselves.

"As long as we continue to search our own hearts for that which doesn't represent God, then we'll always walk within the God potential for our lives."

> For thou hast said in thine heart, I will ascend into heaven; I will exalt my throne above the stars of God: I will sit also upon the mount of the congregation, in the sides of the north. I will ascend above the heights of the clouds; I will be like the Most High. (Isaiah 14:13-14 *KJV*)

What was the sin within the heart of satan? his sin was to exalt himself as king and ruler over God. satan sought to raise his throne *"Authority"* above the throne *"Authority"* of God; satan understood that there could never be two king-doms operating within one another. he also knew there could never be two kings within a kingdom. So if satan understands this principle, then why does church as we've known it still operate within two kingdoms.[96] Remember Jesus said "A house divided against it's self can not stand." See satan was not only seeking recognition; satan was seek-ing supreme authority and rulership over God. Unwilling to submit and humble himself to the authority of God, he then proceeded to try and elevate himself above God. This is an excellent picture that we can use to distinguish the "differ-ence between spiritual fathers and kings."

False Shepherds Are the Same as Kings

Woe to the shepherds of Israel who only take care of themselves! Should not shepherds take care of the flock? You eat the curds, clothe yourselves with the wool and slaughter the choice animals, but you do not take care of the flock. You have not strengthened the weak, or healed the sick or bound up the injured. You have not brought back the strays, or searched for the lost. You have ruled them harshly and brutally. So they were scattered because there was no shepherd, and when they were scattered, they became food for all the wild animals. (Ezekiel 34:1-5 *NIV*)

"We should allow God's word, brought forth out of the mouth of Ezekiel, to continually cause us to walk within the reverent fear of God concerning the raising and releasing of His sons."

This word is as much for today as it was in the time that Ezekiel prophesied it. It's sad, although many ministers all around the world are bringing forth the same results as the shepherds in *Ezekiel 34:1-5*. What was the downfall of the shepherds? Could it have been the acquiring of fame and fortune? Maybe, the shepherds had taken their eyes off of God and had now begun to seek their own well being for personal gain?

How many people do you know that have literally been destroyed by the self-centeredness of men and women within church, as we've known it? These are not the characteristics of a spiritual father but the characteristics of a king. We as the sons of God must first and foremost understand, that *"love and compassion"* are the hallmark of the ministry of Jesus Christ. As fathers, our first and foremost responsibility within the spiritual house is to love as Christ loves. If ever a time comes that you as a minister *"God's delegated representative"* begin to lose your compassion for God's sons and those who are still operating under the law of sin and death, then that is the day the ministry God has entrusted to you, **"DIES"**

> When He saw the crowds He had compassion on them, because they were harassed and helpless, like sheep, without a shepherd. (Matthew 9:36 *NIV*)

"Without love and compassion for others, then we are no longer walking with the heart or nature of Christ."

As spiritual fathers, we must understand that there are consequences to our actions concerning the way in which we raise God's sons. It's time we woke up from this state of complacency and lethargy, which church, as we've known it, has grow accustom to over many generations. My prayer through this book would be that the eyes of your understanding would be enlightened to the truths of God's word. Today our pattern for ministry should be the same pattern that Jesus Christ set for His disciples to follow. As the sons of God, we must continually walk as Christ walked. We'll then begin to see the same results through the outward manifestation of Christ Jesus.

Kings are not interested in walking like Jesus and His disciples. In order for kings to walk as Jesus, they would have to deny themselves and pick up their cross. This is an impossible task for kings to accomplish. I'm not saying *"it's impossible for the hearts of men or women of God who have lost sight of the vision of God, to walk in restoration."* All things are possible with God. I'm saying, *"Once the heart is turned toward God's Divine Order and Godly Government, he or she would no longer remain a king."* There is a difference between spiritual fathers and kings; the difference rests within the motives and attitudes of the heart.

Unlike Kings, Spiritual Fathers release God's Sons

One of the greatest parallels we have concerning a spiritual father loving and releasing the sons of God is found within *Luke 15:11-24.* We are all quite familiar with the story concerning the prodigal son. As we all know the son received his inheritance before his time. The custom of the day was that no son could receive his inheritance prematurely *"Prior to the death of his father."* The father loved his son so much that he was willing to go against the customs of many generations, to freely give all that the son had requested.

After the son had received his inheritance, he quickly squandered it on loose living. The son spent all that his father had given him. The money was gone and there was now a famine in the land. The prodigal son had to rely on eating pods *"that the pigs he was in charge of feeding ate"* in order to survive.

"You could say, "He had reached an all time low. He had hit rock bottom and the only place to go from there was up."

The son began to remember the way the servants were treated in his home. He remembered how they'd always had a good meal on their table. After a time of consideration, the son picked himself up out of the pigpen and decided to go back home to his father and ask for forgiveness. He was hoping his father would allow him to at least work as one of the servants.

As scripture tells, the whole time the lad was gone; his father would continually wait by the side of the road for the return of his lost son. Can you imagine? The people must have thought that the father was crazy, always waiting for his son who chose to live for his inheritance before his time. Finally the long awaited day had arrived. Just as the sun was starting to set, the father saw a shadow of a man up over the horizon and he knew it was his son. As the scripture reads, the father ran and put his arm around him and welcomed him back, not as a servant but as his beloved son.

"There will be times when the spiritual sons decide to leave the spiritual house prematurely; this does not necessarily mean they won't be back."

Sons may leave the spiritual house upon their own decision. As spiritual fathers we must never rule out the truth that God is sovereign. Therefore, through the leading of the Holy Spirit, the sons may return home. It may have been years, since the sons have left the spiritual house. Though if they were truly entrusted by God to His delegated representatives *"Spiritual Fathers"*, then we can never rule out the possibility of their return.

I'm not saying that as spiritual fathers we should forever stay on our knees in prayer, eagerly awaiting their return. This would become detrimental to the rest of the sons within the spiritual house, though there will always be a place in our hearts for the sons that have left prematurely. As fathers, we must come to a place where we can willfully lay the sons *"that God has entrusted to us"* down at His feet. This relates to those who are presently within the spiritual house, as well as those who have left the spiritual house prematurely or with the fathers blessing. Sons are ultimately responsible for their own actions. The spiritual father is only responsible and held accountable by God, for the way in which he or she has raised and equipped the sons of God to do the work of ministry.

> But the father said to the servant, quick bring the best robe and put it on him! Put a ring on his finger and sandals on his feet. Bring the fatted calf and kill it. Let's have a feast and celebrate. For this son of mine was dead and now is alive, he was lost and now is found, so they began to celebrate. (Luke 15:22-24 *NIV*)

We've learned within this passage of scripture, that the prodigal son had received a robe and a ring upon his return. Though there was one more significant item that was given to the son from his father, *"New sandals."* The new sandals or new shoes represent the fact that the father had now given his son the ability to leave once again upon his own free will. We can see that the father loved his son unconditionally. The father was ready to prove his love, by giving his son the ability to leave once again.

We need to understand that a true spiritual father will never try to keep God's sons within the confines of the spiritual house. Only kings use manipulation and control in order to try and keep the sons within their kingdoms. As spiritual fathers we should love and take great joy in seeing the sons that have been entrusted to our care released from the spiritual house, once they have reached maturity. Remember that spiritual fathers are only as successful as their spiritual sons.

"Without the releasing of spiritual sons, spiritual fathers would deny the sown seed the ability to reproduce after its own kind".

Kings Never Release

Many of us are familiar with the story of Joseph the son of Jacob and Rachel. It was no secret among all the brothers that Joseph was favored by Jacob more then any other son. Joseph was sold into slavery, after sharing a dream with his brothers, *"concerning the fact that they would one day bow down before him."* Joseph was a strong-willed child, one with solid character concerning the things of God. After he was sold into slavery, he eventually found himself in Potiphars's house, where after refusing to lay with Potiphars's wife, was accused of rape. As the result of her accusation, Joseph was then sentenced to prison. Although the events within Joseph's life seemed quite drastic, they continued to build the character of God within Joseph. Joseph knew who his God was and what it meant to walk within the reverent fear of the Lord. While in prison he never stopped believing in the dream the Lord had given him, the dream concerning Joseph's brothers bowing down at his feet. The word of God tells us that Joseph won the favor of Pharaoh through correctly interpreting his dream. Through the obedience of Joseph unto the Lord, God gave Joseph the interpretation of Pharaoh's dream and as a result Joseph was placed in charge over of the whole land of Egypt.

> Then Pharaoh took his signet ring from his finger and put it on Joseph's finger. He dressed him in robes of fine linen and put a gold chain around his neck. (Genesis 41:42 *NIV*)

To most people Joseph's reward would seem like a pretty good deal though we must look at the difference of the reward given by a king to his or her sons, as opposed to the reward a spiritual father gives to his or her spiritual sons. All aspects sound the same concerning the reward of the prodigal son and Joseph. Both received a ring on their finger, which represents, "Covenant, *belonging to a family*." We also see that both the prodigal son and Joseph received robes of royalty. So what was the difference in the last gift given to each? The difference was in the sandals, or shoes. Pharaoh gave Joseph material things "gold *chain*", instead of shoes. The shoes would have empowered him to go and come as he pleased. Joseph was confined to the land of Egypt; though he had the appearance of freedom, he was still a slave.

"Kings will never release the sons that are under them. Without the sons there would be no wind in which the kings could continue to elevate themselves upon."

The most important key in this chapter is the fact that spiritual fathers love and release spiritual sons. Fathers have only the best interest in mind for the sons of God. Kings rule their sons out of their own selfish desires. Kings only love and care for their sons if everything is going as they'd planned. There is no room for kings in God's Divine Order and Godly Government. *It's time we asked ourselves this question.*

"Who am I, a spiritual father or a king?"

CHAPTER EIGHT

Jesus Fathers His Disciples "Spiritual Sons"

As we've now come to the last chapter within this book, it's only fitting to bring out the true structural pattern for spiritual fathers. This true pattern is found within the life of Jesus Christ and His relationship with the disciples. Within this chapter we'll see the shocking characteristics of a spiritual father, portrayed by Jesus "Son of Man." This type of understanding is necessary for the restoration and reforming of the Church of Jesus Christ back to Divine Order and Godly Government.

Within this chapter, we'll see how Jesus Christ raised His sons "*Disciples*." Through *teaching, instructing, equipping, loving, correcting, speaking destiny and releasing His sons into ministry*. I trust that the Holy Spirit will open your eyes and ears in order to allow you to see and hear the truth within this chapter. This chapter was designed to bring validity to all that we have discussed within this book. Jesus was much more then a teacher to His disciples. Jesus was even more then a tutor to His disciples. As well, Jesus was much more then an instructor or friend to His disciples.

Jesus was a *"spiritual father"* to His *"spiritual sons"* disciples. Let's now take a look at the first father-son relationship concerning the new generation, *"The sons of God."*

Characteristics and Preparations of Spiritual Fathers

As spiritual fathers, we must humble ourselves before the sons of God, never elevating ourselves in the natural above others, in the name of ministry. Jesus *"while allowing John the Baptist to baptize Him in the waters of the Jordan,"* was our best example of humbling oneself before others.[97] Jesus came with a servant's heart, in order to reach those who were hurting.

"Jesus was called to serve no man, but God alone though In order for Jesus to serve God, He first had to become a servant of man."

It's important to understand that spiritual fathers must follow this simple principle. As fathers, we must first serve God, and through our service unto God, become servants to God's sons that have been entrusted to us. Therefore we must become good stewards of God's sons. Remember that as the hearts of the fathers are turned, the desire for spiritual sons will increase. Only through a genuine desire birth out of the heart of God will spiritual fathers qualify to raise the sons of God, once our hearts are turned, so is our understanding and long term vision concerning God's plan, purpose and design for the future. It's at this point *"Turning of the heart"* that we are approved to raise the sons of God. We receive the approval of God, before the first son is ever entrusted to us.

As Jesus came up from the waters of baptism, the Spirit of God "the Holy Spirit" descended upon Him like a dove. Then the Lord spoke, and His voice was heard. *"This is my beloved Son in Whom I am well pleased."* Even though

Jesus had not yet begun His ministry, Father God had already given Him His seal of approval. God is only concerned with the heart. Jesus had already gone to Calvary within His heart, in His heart; the work had already taken place.[98] Jesus had loved the unlovely and hugged the unhugable. Jesus' heart had already been prepared to receive the sons of God. He was ready to become a spiritual father, before He had received His first son "Disciple."

Tried By Fire
Upon the approval of the ministry of Jesus Christ, had now come a testing that was necessary. This passed test would further make the man "Jesus" for the ministry. Jesus was now entering into what so many of us go through right after a great victory, *"The Wilderness."* [99] It's necessary for spiritual fathers to receive testing, as to the work of the heart on the inside. Don't worry about the testing of the Lord. If we have truly allowed our hearts to be turned to receive God's sons, then as spiritual fathers we'll pass the test. Fathers will be tested in many different ways. Remember that God does not deal with each person the same way, though His ultimate results are always the same.

This is why it's very important to recognize the times of testing so we'll be able to pass with flying colors. We must start to look at every thing that comes our way with the eyes of God, whether good or bad. Remember, *"All things work for good to those who love the Lord and are called according to His purpose."* While in the wilderness we need to continue to have an ear to hear what the spirit is saying.

Keep in mind that the very thing that brings death is also need in order to bring forth life. As we begin to die to our own selfish desires of the flesh, we'll begin to rise and walk a new life in Christ. God will test spiritual fathers though if we remain focused upon the call of God for holiness and righteous living, we'll surely pass His test.

Jesus Teaches His Disciple "Spiritual Sons"

As spiritual fathers, we're required to teach the sons of God. Throughout this chapter we'll discuss many responsibilities of the spiritual father. One of the most important responsibilities of a father is to teach God's sons. The outcome of the spiritual sons will rely on the fathers' ability to teach. Jesus proves this responsibility of a spiritual father to be true.

> As Jesus was walking beside the Sea of Galilee, He saw two brothers Simon called Peter and his brother Andrew. They were casting their net, for they were fishermen. "Come follow me" Jesus said and I will make you fishers of men. (Matthew 4:18-19 *NIV*)

Jesus said "*Come follow me and I will make you fishers of men.*" The key word within this scripture is "*make.*" We need to understand that Jesus did not command His disciples to follow Him. He simply called out their destiny, though they still had a choice whether to except or reject the call of the Lord. There were others that Jesus called to follow Him, though they counted the cost and decided the price was too high to pay.[100]

Jesus understood the responsibility that lay before Him, the responsibility of raising the sons of God. He was prepared to fashion and mold His disciples into mighty men of God. Have you ever made something at least once in your life? If so, then you will understand that making something and assembling something are two totally different works. In order to make something, you are required to place a part of yourself into whatever you are making. Therefore the desire to see your project come to life is revealed within the very presentation of the project you are working on. This

was the very understanding Jesus had, the understanding
that He was responsible for pouring His life into the lives of
His disciples "*Spiritual Sons*."

Spiritual fathers need to understand that we carry this
same responsibility, *"called to make sons of God."* We must
also pour our whole lives *"In Christ"* into the lives of those
God has entrusted us to raise and then release. The very act of
fatherhood is to reproduce offspring. We learn through scripture that the Disciples of Jesus were obedient to the call,
forsaking all for Christ. [101] This is an important qualification
for all spiritual sons. Remember that children within the
"*Spiritual House*" are those who have not yet caught the
vision or plan of God. They are those who continue to walk
with the attitude, *"I am just a saint saved by grace."* These
individuals would not be considered spiritual sons, for they
continually remove their hand from the plow and look back.
Therefore, the father within the spiritual house would have no
true authority to make them disciples. Remember the father
never goes looking for the sons. Christ joins the spiritual sons
to the spiritual father, through the unction of the Holy Spirit.

Spiritual fathers will always minister to the multitudes;
though they are equipping spiritual sons to do the work of
ministry.[102] Though Jesus was teaching the disciples "Sons,"
He was scattering seed for the multitudes into many different
types of soil. Jesus taught the disciples many things concerning the Kingdom of God. Jesus taught His disciples to
develop a relationship with their Heavenly Father, "through
prayer." [103] Jesus also taught His disciple how to establish an
"intimate relationship" with their Heavenly Father.[104]

He taught His disciples the power of the spoken word,
and the necessity for establishing the principle of team
ministry. [105] We need to understand that God's order has
never called His body to operate as a one-man ministry. This
structural pattern has only produced kings instead of fathers,
in Church, as we've known it. Team ministry is necessary in

order to allow the body of Christ to remain accountable to one another. While feeding the multitude, Jesus asked the disciples to give them something to eat.[106] We need to see the pattern that Jesus was establishing with the disciples. As spiritual fathers, we must begin to allow the sons of God the ability to function within the gifts of the Holy Spirit. There is no safer place to practice operating within the gifts, than in the "Spiritual House." There must come a time of hands on training for the sons of God.

As spiritual fathers, we must first become the living example and then allow the sons to begin walking within the same patterns. Jesus taught His disciples "Sons" by example concerning the authority needed to cast out unclean spirits.[107] Also scripture tells how Jesus taught His disciples to serve, through becoming a living example.[108] Through the washing of the disciple's feet, Jesus was teaching a spiritual truth. The truth was that as sons of God, we must never forget that we are first servants to mankind. We're servants of the gospel of love and forgiveness as well as compassion and grace. Through Jesus' act of servant hood, the disciples learned what true love was.

Though Jesus taught the disciples how to love, nothing could compare to a living illustration.[109] Jesus openly conveyed the love of God to His sons "Disciples." This allowed an entrance to open up within their hearts, so that He could share the plan of Father God with them. Once their hearts were prepared, Jesus could then reveal the plan of eternal salvation for all mankind, not just His disciples'.[110]

Teaching is one of the most important tools we as spiritual fathers need, in order to raise the sons of God to do the works of ministry. As fathers, no matter what five-fold office you have been called to, the Holy Spirit has already given you the ability to raise, equip and release God's sons. This means that through the Holy Spirit, you now have the ability to teach spiritual sons, in the ways of the Lord.

Instructing Spiritual Sons

Just like Jesus, we as spiritual fathers have the responsibility to teach. We also carry the responsibility of instructing the sons of God. Instruction is different then teaching. Unfortunately they have both been placed within the same category. To instruct is the ability to take what has already been taught and begin to channel it into a certain direction. Instruction will lead the way to a result *"Finished product"*, for that which we already have knowledge about. Jesus taught His disciples and then instructed them, as to the way they should handle different situations.

> I am sending you out like sheep among wolves, therefore be as shrewd as snakes and as innocent as doves. (Matthew 10:17 *NIV*)

It's important within this next segment that we gain the understanding of the difference between teaching and instructing. We can learn throughout the ministry of Jesus that He not only taught His disciples but instructed them as well. One example is when Jesus was teaching His disciples concerning false Prophets. Jesus gave specific instruction how to deal with them.[111] Jesus also instructed His disciples to obey the law or government of man, *"outside the structural order of God's Government for His Church."* Jesus instructed them to obey the law concerning tax; [112] *"Give unto Ceaser what is Ceaser', and give unto God what is God's."* Jesus had also instructed His disciples concerning the religion and tradition of man. [113]

Teaching is one of the most important functional roles of the spiritual father though all the teaching in the world remains powerless without instruction.

If I gave you tools to build a house, though you were

never instructed on how to use the tools. It would be safe to say that the structural blueprint of the house would not be built properly. Without proper instruction concerning the usage of the tools, then the only thing we'd create would be a counterfeit. Though a counterfeit may have to some extent the image of what is *"true,"* it's still *"deception."* We need to understand that men and women have been building church, as we've known it for many years, with the right tools but without godly instruction on how to build. Therefore many organizations within church, as we've known it, have only created a counterfeit of the true Church of Jesus Christ, *"Having a form of structure though incapable of walking in God's Divine Order and Godly Government."*

Imparting Into the Lives of Spiritual Sons

Along side teaching and instructing, there is yet another important functional role of fatherhood. We as fathers must release an impartation into the lives of God's sons, through the inspiration of the Holy Spirit. Fathers must be lead and guided directly by the Holy Spirit. We as five-fold ministers "God's delegated Representatives" lack the power to raise and properly equip spiritual sons, as long as we continue to deny within our own lives, the existence and life-giving power of the Holy Spirit.

Impartation must first take place within the heart of the spiritual father. Only then are we capable of imparting the life of Christ into the hearts of the spiritual sons. Impartation *"Is the ability to receive and walk within the power and demonstration of the life of Christ, revealed through the word."* As five-fold ministers, we have no God-given right to minister without continually receiving the impartation of the Holy Spirit. Therefore, if we deny the abilities of the Holy Spirit within our own lives, then we'll instill those same values into the lives of the spiritual sons. We'd then be held responsible for creating or reproducing seedless offspring, men and women that have been denied the ability to receive the power of God need to manifest His Kingdom on earth. Though having the appearance of a fully functional son, they are really only "*eunuchs*."

We've seen through scripture that Jesus imparts understanding and the God vision into the lives of His disciples'.[114] We've also seen how Jesus through the act of servant hood, brought forth an impartation into the lives of His disciples.[115] We need to remember that Jesus would always minister to the multitude though Jesus would always impart the truths into the lives of His disciples at a later time. Teaching, instructing and impartation are three major keys in order to successfully father spiritual sons "*God's sons*." These are the very responsibilities that Jesus had taken upon Himself, in order to properly raise, equip, and release the disciples into ministry. As fathers and fathers to be, we must not fail to see and follow the structural pattern of Jesus. The life of Jesus Christ is vital to the advancement of the Kingdom of God through Spiritual fathers and sons. What was good for the disciples at the start of the New Testament is good enough for spiritual sons today.

Greatest Quality of a Spiritual Father Is Love

> Love the Lord your God with all of your heart
> and with all your soul and with all your mind.
> This is the first and greatest commandment.
> And the second is like it; love your neighbor
> like yourself. (Matthew 22:37-39 *NIV*)

Without love we are no more than a resounding gong and a clanging cymbal.[116] As fathers, we must first and foremost love as Christ loves. Only love can qualify spiritual fathers to raise spiritual sons. As spiritual fathers, we must begin to open up and allow through love, relationships to develop within the lives of "spiritual sons." Love is the only fruit that qualifies all believers to walk within the manifested presence of God.

Spiritual fathers must never portray that they are functioning at a level that is impossible for the spiritual sons to attain, or even surpass. As we begin to share our hearts with sons, we must present ourselves upon the different levels of the sons. We need to always remember to remain real. If not, then once again the sons will follow in the pattern that was established for them. This type of a pattern will only lead to loneliness and misery within the lives of the spiritual sons. As spiritual fathers, we must remain honest with God's sons that have been entrusted to us. Though we may not share everything we know with them, though when we do share, we need to remain honest and real within that situation.

As we begin to love the spiritual sons, then we release the power to tear down all walls. Love will tear down all walls within the lives of every believer, including the spiritual sons. Love as well covers a multitude of sin.[117] Jesus showed us the pattern of pure unconditional love, while willingly allowing violent men to nail His hands and feet down to an emblem of suffering and shame, "The tree of death." [118] I know we have heard it said before, though it's worth repeating.

"It wasn't the nails that held our savior suspended between heaven and earth, but His love for you and I."

As Christians *"Christ-like"* we're called to become imitators of Christ, though the only true way to imitate Christ is to love unconditionally as Christ loves.[119] Remember that love is the root of all things, everything stems from the fruit of love. The gifts of the spirit or the anointing can never be the trademark or hallmark of Christ. Though the true nature and character of Christ is love, *"How will they know you, by your love for one another?"* Only through our willingness to allow the Holy Spirit to have complete control over our will, can we ever love as Christ loves. Therefore, in order to become an imitator of Christ, we must live a spirit led and directed lifestyle.

Jesus loved His disciples as a natural father would love his children.[120] The love of Jesus flowed from His heart, as He sought the well being of His disciples. Jesus also showed great love for those who had not yet been born in the natural and for those that were naturally born, that would one day receive Him as Lord and King. As spiritual fathers, we need to have both a strong love for the spiritual sons and for the rest of the world as well. Remember God will give those who ask, *"The nations as their inheritance."*

> Come to me all you who are weary and burdened and I will give you rest. Take my yoke upon you and learn from me. For I am gentle and humble in heart, and you will find rest for your souls. For my yoke is easy, and my burden is light. (Matthew 11:28-30 *NIV*)

"The life of Jesus is our pattern for becoming an imitator of Christ."

As spiritual fathers begin to walk within the love of Christ, we'll then become like Christ, *"Humble and Gentle in heart."* Many times in scripture we've seen where Jesus would comfort His disciples and speak peace into their lives, seeming to always calm their storm.[121]

It's important to understand that spiritual fathers are not only called to show forth love and comfort when raising spiritual sons. They must also show compassion. We have learned through the ministry of Jesus Christ that He always had compassion on others.[122] We must understand that it was the power of Christ that allowed Jesus to walk within love, comfort and compassion. Outside of the Christ nature, Jesus would have been powerless to affect the hearts of men and women through love, comfort and compassion. Remember that Jesus "son of man" represented humanity. Though the Christ within Jesus represented the all knowing, all powerful, all present God. Jesus had become the most ultimate example of love while upon the cross, that this world had ever seen. The very words are still to this day echoing throughout the universe, *"Father forgive them, for they know not what they do."* [123] As spiritual fathers, we must lay down our own lives first, in order for the spiritual sons to truly live as Christ lives. We must become obedient vessels faithfully walking and being led by God's spirit. Without faithful vessels, then the world must continue to wait for another generation that'll be willing to restore Christ's true Church back to Divine Order and Godly Government.

Spiritual Fathers Must Correct Their Spiritual Sons

> My son do not make light on the Lords discipline and do not lose heart when He rebukes you, because the Lord disciplines those whom He loves and He punishes everyone He excepts as a son.(Hebrews 12:5-6 NIV)

> Because the Lord disciplines those He loves, as a father the son He delights in. (Proverbs 3:12 *NIV*)

As spiritual fathers within a spiritual house, we're responsible for seeing that God's Divine Order and Godly Government remains consistent within the lives of the sons. Correction and rebuke within a spiritual house are necessary, in order to properly establish God's true structural order for His Church. Correction and rebuke should only be brought forth from the spiritual father or fathers within the spiritual family "house." Remember that it's not the elders or the spiritual sons' function to correct one another or the saints' "children," though it is their function to show forth love and compassion. Correction and rebuke should always be brought forth out of a heart of love and never to tear down individuals, but to build, encourage and exalt one another. Correction and rebuke if brought forth out of love, is never a negative within the body of Christ. Without correction and rebuke, there would be no true growth and development within the spiritual sons of the house.

If fathers correct or rebuke God's sons with any other motive then to build, encourage, and exalt, then we are out of order. As the body of Christ, we must stop condemning one another. We must start to build one another up in the most holy of faith. Correction is necessary, though only when brought forth out of love, will it produce life.

Jesus rebuked Peter for his lack of understanding but then imparted into his life spiritual truth.[124] Scriptures also show Jesus openly rebuking His disciples.' [125] Understand that correction and rebuke is necessary in order to establish the character and nature of Christ within the lives of both men and women. Correction and rebuke teaches sons to walk in submission and authority in Christ. As we have discussed within chapter four, "Eli's sons of unrestraint" spiritual sons must submit to the authority of Christ within a spiritual father. We must keep submission and authority within the right perspective," *the God perspective.*"

There is no one great or small within the Kingdom of God. Those who have been redeemed by the blood of the lamb have now become sons of God. Understand that we must walk first as sons, before we can become fathers. Notice we are not saying that we must walk first as saints. Saints are the children within a spiritual house. As children, they have not yet caught the vision and submitted to the hand of God within the spiritual father or fathers. Therefore, they are not considered to be spiritual sons. Though their hearts could turn toward the spiritual father, in which a spiritual son would be born.

Speaking Destiny into the Disciples

We read in chapter three "Hannah's Cry" concerning the fact that we as spiritual fathers are required to speak into the destiny of those who had been entrusted to us by God. As destiny is spoken, we'll begin to see life come forth through the hearts of the spiritual sons. As we begin to speak destiny, God's word will begin to bring life to the plans of God, which have lay dormant since birth.

Just as a plow tills the hard and stubborn ground, in order to cause the ground to produce fruit, so does the word of God once spoken within our hearts. We need to grasp this simple principle, and begin to operate in it. As we do, we'll begin to see life flow throughout the spiritual house, flowing up, and out of the spiritual sons. For it's this life that causes the sons of God to begin walking in their God-given destiny. Understand that as fathers we are nothing more then the catalyst used by God to launch His sons into their greater destiny. As fathers, we are called to lead and direct God's sons into their God-given destiny. Fathers will know the direction to lead each son, as long as we continue to have an ear to hear what the spirit is saying.

On many different occasions Jesus spoke destiny into the lives of His disciples. Sometimes destiny was spoken one-on-one. At different times destiny was spoken to individuals. Nevertheless, Jesus was aware of the responsibility He had been given by God. Jesus was responsible for speaking forth destiny into God's sons. Jesus spoke destiny when He said, *"Follow me and I will make you fishers of men."* [126] The Christ on the inside of Jesus was calling forth destiny.

Christ still works today, in the hearts of spiritual fathers the same way. As fathers, we call forth the destiny of all men and women through ministering to the multitude, though only the sons respond.

Jesus spoke destiny into Peter's life.[127] Jesus called Peter blessed, which refers to the approval of Jesus. God had just revealed to Peter that Jesus was the Christ, the Son of the living God. See Peter was developing right heart motives and right heart attitudes. Through these developments, Peter was able to receive the revelation of the Christ, *"The Anointed One"* from God. Without the willing heart of Peter, Jesus would have had no ability to speak God destiny within his heart. Once spiritual sons begin to worship out of their heart, as well as minister and serve from their heart, we as spiritual fathers will receive the release from God to entrust the spiritual sons with godly revelation and understanding.

We have learned through scripture, the fact that Jesus had spoken concerning His own destiny. [128] Though His destiny directly related to the destiny of each disciple, "Sons." Fathers must relay the God vision that we have been entrusted with, to the spiritual sons. As the sons catch the vision, God's greater work, birthed in the fathers, will continue to be accomplished. Not all-spiritual fathers will carry the same vision, though the vision of each individual father, works together for one main purpose, to build and advance the Kingdom of God.

Sons are not joined by chance to a gift of God. The fact that a particular son of God is joined and jointed to a spiritual father portrays the heart and destiny the spiritual son is called to walk in. Therefore the son will walk with the same heart as the father, even thought they may both walk in two totally different responsibilities and even functional offices. We must see the need to speak into the heart of sons, in order to bring forth change.

Jesus Releases His Disciples "Spiritual Sons"

We have learned that Hannah raised Samuel and then released him to minister unto the Lord all the days of his life. This is a natural picture of Hannah and her son, which we as spiritual fathers must relate to, concerning spiritual sons. The responsibility of releasing; is truly a vital part in God's testing, in order to distinguish who are true spiritual fathers. Remember, only kings are against the releasing of their sons. It should always be a pleasure for the spiritual father to bring forth the release of God's sons. Jesus has provided this wonderful pattern for spiritual fathers. We learn through scripture that Jesus would send His disciples out two by two.[129] Not only was Jesus presenting or establishing a pattern for releasing, though he was also establishing a pattern in which they went out. Jesus was teaching both the importance and necessity of team ministry within the body of Christ. We know that Jesus released more then twelve disciples to do the work of ministry.[130] Jesus had also released the seventy, in order to do the work of ministry.

> Go into all the world and preach the good news to all creation, whoever believes and is baptized will be saved, but whoever does not believe will be condemned. And these signs will accompany those who believe; in my name they will drive out demons, they will speak in new tongues, they will pick up snakes with their hands, and when the drink deadly poison, it will not hurt them at all. They will place their hands on the sick people, and they shall recover. (Mark 16:15-19 *NIV*)

There are many more scriptures to validate the pattern Jesus used for releasing His disciples to do the work of ministry. I'd like to encourage you to begin looking them up and asking the Holy Spirit to reveal His truths.

Jesus Had Different Levels of Relationship

We see continually within the ministry of Jesus that He developed different types of relationships with His disciples, "*SONS*." This is the one true pattern that we as spiritual fathers can't afford to not follow. Fathers have a greater responsibility to the spiritual sons concerning relationship, then they have to the saints "children" within the ministry. As spiritual fathers, we need to recognize the difference between the responsibilities of a spiritual son and the responsibilities of a saint within the spiritual house. Spiritual fathers will always minister to the saints of the house, though as fathers we can only raise, equip, and release the spiritual sons. There will be a difference between the relationships a spiritual father has with the spiritual sons as opposed to the saints in the ministry. We must draw a line of distinction between the two. Without a firm understanding of both spiritual sons and saints, fathers would spend all their time trying to energize the ones that never want to be energized. This type of labor proves to be very costly to the gift of God "God's delegated Representatives." As fathers, we're only capable of raising "*making*" the sons of God that have been entrusted to us. Though if we start looking to recruit spiritual sons on our own, we will only produce the sons of man.

As spiritual sons, we'll walk within different levels of relationship with the spiritual father. Each relationship depends on the heart, the call of God and functional role that each individual son walks in. We see that even among the disciples, Jesus shared a deeper relationship with Peter, James, and John. We also learn within the ministry of Jesus, that he had different relationships with the twelve, the seventy and the one hundred and twenty.

"If there is one thing that will start healing our nations, its true heart-shared relationships one with another."

I know that this book has stretched our tent pegs. I find myself asking the same question over and over again. *"Is it possible to stop this mechanical machine called church, long enough to establish God's true Divine Order and Godly Government?"*

The truth is that we can't, but God can. We need only to let go of the old and embrace Christ Jesus the hope of glory.

Endnotes

Chapter One

[1] 1 John 2: 18-29 (They went out from us, but the really didn't know us)

[2] Genesis 2:7 (Creation of man)

[3] John 4:24 (God is spirit)

[4] 1 Thessalonians 5:23 (May your whole spirit, soul and body remain blameless)

[5] Ezekiel 28:14 (Thou art the anointed cherub, King James Version)

[6] Proverbs 2:7-8 (Confirms Jobs protection by God for his upright living)

[7] Psalm 37:25 (God has never forsaken the righteous)

[8] 1Corinthians 10:26 (The earth and everything in it belongs to God)

[9] Job 42:12-16 (God was testing Job for promotion)

[10] Genesis 15 (Establishing the Abrahamic Covenant)

[11] Romans 8:9-11 (Believers have the Christ nature dwelling within them)

[12] Ephesians 5:25-27 (Spotless without sin)

[13] 1Kings 11:1-3 (Natural picture of being fruitful and

multiplying)

14 Romans 6:10 (Jesus Christ died once and for all)

15 Romans 10:9-10 (We must accept Jesus Christ as our sacrifice)

16 1 Corinthians 11:25 (Blood Covenant)

17 Acts 1:8 (Baptism of Holy Spirit)
Matthew 3:11 (Baptism of Christ "fire")

18 Isaiah 51:3 (Joy and gladness will be found within Zion, Zion will be strengthened and anointed) (Joy of the Lord is our strength, oil of gladness instead of mourning)

Chapter 2

19 Daniel 12:4 (Ever increasing knowledge)

20 Ephesians 1:10, 3:15 (God's Government is to establish family)

21 2 Peter 3:9

22 1 Corinthians 7 (Spiritual grounds for divorce)

23 Genesis 2:18 (Complement one another and bring balance to the relationship)

24 Proverbs 1:8 (Mothers teach) 31:20 (Loving and nurturing)
Proverbs 31:26 (Speaking wisdom) 31:27 (Mothers are protective)
Psalm 22:9 (Natural instilled form of nurturing)

25 Hebrews 12:8-9, 5-6 (Fathers bring correction)
Proverbs 3:12 (Fathers pattern their lives after God / instill values to children)

26 Proverbs 4:1-4 (Father Instruction to sound doctrine brings understanding)
Matthew 7:15-27 (Jesus Christ laid the foundation for true fatherhood)

27 1 Timothy 5:8 (Both parents are held accountable for raising their children)

28 Matthew 4:19 (I will make you fishers of men) 16:13-20 (Destiny of Peter)
    Mark 8:31-38 (Jesus spoke concerning His destiny, for the disciples)
29 Genesis 3:16, 1 Corinthians 11:3 (Husband second only to God's authority)
30 Ephesians 4:11-16 (Gift's given to the Church by God)
31 Elders (Strong's Exhaustive Concordance # 4245) member of a celestial council
    Governing Elders: Men and women called and appointed by God to functional office of an Apostle, prophet, evangelist, pastor or teacher.
    General Elders: Men and women recognized for their wisdom and maturity in the word. Assisting God's delegated representatives *"Spiritual Father or Fathers"* Overseeing the spiritual matters of the spiritual house through teaching, instructing and continually speaking and keeping God's vision for His people alive within their hearts on a daily basis.
32 Matthew 6:5-14 (Jesus taught His disciples to pray), 22:37 (Love the Father)
    Matthew 14:13-21 (Teaches team ministry)
    Mark 4:35-41 (Power of the spoken word)
33 John 15:4, 7 (Christ is the word)
34 1Corinthians 1:2, Ephesians 1:1
35 Matthew 11:28-30 (Jesus compassion) John 17 (love for disciples-sons)

Chapter 3

36 1 Samuel 1:6-8
37 1 Samuel 1:11
38 Genesis 30:1
39 Genesis 29:31-35

[40] Malachi 4:5-6
[41] John 17:20-22
[42] Luke 1:31-33 (Christ Reigns Supreme)
[43] 1 Timothy 3:8-12 (Deacons were allowed wine/ Priesthood wasn't)
      Act 6:1-7 (Deacons were appointed to handle natural matters)
[44] Matthew 16:13-20 (Christ our King is called to build His Church, You and I)
[45] 1 Samuel 1:11
[46] 1 Peter 2:9-10 (Holy Nation)
[47] 1 Samuel 2:18-20 (Priestly garment)
[48] Matthew 16:17-19 (Jesus spoke destiny into the life of Peter)
[49] Galatians 3:26 (Sons of God)
[50] 1 Corinthians 12:11 (As He will's)
[51] Romans 8:14 (Led by the spirit)
[52] 1 Corinthians 12:4-7 (Every believer walks in the gifts and anointing of God,
      (Though gifting and anointing alone, will never make a man or women of God)
[53] 2 Corinthians 5:17-18 (Ministry of Christ Jesus)
[54] 1 Corinthians 3:5-9 (Some plant, some water, God brings the increase)
[55] Luke 10:1-12 (Jesus sent out the seventy)

Chapter 4   *No Endnotes*

Chapter 5

[56] Hebrews 3:1 (Jesus Chief Apostle)
[57] Isaiah 52:1-3 (Zion dwelling place of God in the spirit)
[58] Romans 5:8

59 Hebrews 9:12-14, John 3:16 (God's Blood)
60 Romans 8:29, Revelation 21:3-9
61 Galatians 2:20-21
62 John 14:6-7 (Way, truth, life)
63 John 1:1-2
64 Exodus 18:13-27 (Jethro Principle)
65 Ephesians 2:20
66 1 Corinthians 3:10-15
67 Matthew 4:19-20, Acts 9:1-9

Chapter 6

In regards to material listing 30AD through 380AD was provided with consent by Apostle Dave Viljoen Founder of Apostolic Working Company. Reference material was derived from school of ministry notes.

68 Proverbs 8:6-9 (Speak what is right)
69 Proverbs 20:3, Proverbs 25:28
70 James 1:19
71 Ezekiel 34:1-5
72 2 Samuel 6:1-11
73 2 Chronicles 7:14
74 1 Corinthians 15:53
75 1 Corinthians 2:16
76 Acts 9:4-6
77 1 Thessalonians 2:6-12
78 Hebrews 10: 25
79 Mark 7:13
80 Luke 1:32-33

Chapter 7

81 Luke 17:20-23 (There is only one kingdom and one king, "KING JESUS")
82 Matthew 24:10-11 (False Prophets) Mark 13:22-23 (False Christ's)
2 Corinthians 11:12-15 (False Apostles) 2 Timothy 3:1-9 (False Teachers)
83 Matthew 23:25 (Appearance of godliness)
84 Matthew 7:15-20 (Know them by their fruits)
85 Romans 3:23 (All have fallen short of God's glory)
86 John 10:14 (I am the good shepherd)
87 Mark 1:17 (I will "MAKE")
88 Proverbs 4:1 (Fathers must raise children), 17:6 (Fathers cover their children)
89 Romans 1:21-25 (Started pure in heart / wound up corrupt)
90 Luke 7:7-10 (Must submit to natural and spiritual authority)
91 2 Corinthians 4:18 (Keep our focus solely upon the Lord)
92 1 John 4:8 (God is Love), 4: 16 (He that dwells in love dwells in God)
93 1 Timothy 6:10 (The love of money is corrupt)
94 1 Samuel 8:19-20
95 Matthew 7:24-29 (Building upon a corrupt foundation)
96 Mark 3:24-26 (House divided against itself can not stand)

Chapter 8

97 Matthew 3:13-17 (Jesus humbled Himself before John the Baptist and others)
98 Matthew 3:17 (The approval of the ministry of Jesus Christ)

[99] Matthew 4:1-11 (Tested for 40 days within the wilderness)
[100] Matthew 10:17-31 (Forsake all) Luke 9:57-62 (Don't look back)
[101] Matthew 4:20-22 (Forsake all in order to follow Christ)
[102] Matthew 5:1-12 (Jesus ministered to the multitude, though taught His disciples)
[103] Matthew 6:5-15 (Jesus taught His disciples to pray)
[104] Matthew 22:37-38 (All your heart, soul and mind)
[105] Matthew 14:13-21 (Team ministry)
[106] Matthew 14:16 (Jesus wanted the disciple to minister, "serve" the multitude)
[107] Mark 1:21-28 (Jesus taught His disciples how to deal with unclean spirits)
[108] John 13:3-7 (Jesus teaches the disciples servant hood)
[109] Luke 22:39-46 (Mount of Olives)
[110] Luke 14:25-27 (Jesus loved His disciples) John 5:19-47
[111] Matthew 7:15-23 (Jesus instructs His disciples)
[112] Matthew 22:15-22 (Jesus instructs concerning obeying governmental laws)
[113] Matthew 23:1-39 (Jesus teaches and instructs concerning religion and tradition)
[114] Mark 4:13-20 (Jesus imparts God vision)
[115] Mark 9:35 (Impartation into the lives of the disciples through servant hood)
[116] 1 Corinthians 13:1 (All things stem from love)
[117] James 5:20, 1 Peter 4:8 (Love covers a multitude of sin)
[118] John 3:16 (Unconditional love)
[119] Ephesians 5:1-2 (Imitators of Christ)
[120] John 17: ALL (Jesus displayed great love for His disciples)
[121] Matthew 14:27 (Take courage) John 14:1-4 (I won't leave you fatherless)
[122] Luke 23:43 (The compassion of Christ towards others)
[123] Luke 23:34 (No greater love)

[124] Matthew 16: All (Jesus rebuked Peter)

[125] Mark 4:40 (Open rebuke among the disciples)

[126] Matthew 4:19 (Jesus speaks destiny into the sons of God)

[127] Matthew 16:13-20 (Jesus speaks destiny into Peter's life)

[128] Mark 8:31-38 (Jesus spoke His destiny, which relates to His disciple's destiny)

[129] Mark 6:6-12 (Jesus released His disciples, "Spiritual Sons")

[130] Luke 10:1-23 (Jesus sets a pattern of releasing His sons and team ministry)

Contact Information: paulgraves@bibletolife.com

Bible to Life Ministries
Atlanta, Georgia
www.bibletolifeministries.com

Lightning Source UK Ltd.
Milton Keynes UK
UKOW041848201212

203968UK00001B/24/A